JESUS CHRIST

*The Love and Wisdom
of a 1st Century Mystic*

Isabella Price

ONE TRUTH MANY PATHS

FIRST EDITION
Copyright © 2014 by Isabella Price
Published by One Truth Many Paths
www.onetruth-manypaths.com

All rights reserved. No part of this book may be reproduced in any form, excerpt brief excerpts for the purpose of review, without the express permission of the publisher.

ISBN: 978-0-9908564-6-7

Library of Congress Control Number:
2014955850

Book Design & Typography:
D. Patrick Miller
www.fearlessbooks.com/Literary.html

Cover Art: *Christ's Face*, a modern mosaic in Byzantine style by an unknown Sicilian artist. Procured copyright-free via Shutterstock.

CONTENTS

- viii • Acknowledgments
- 1 • Introduction to the Series
- 12 • An Overview of Christianity within a Cross-Cultural Context
- 19 • Early Sources of Information About the Historical Jesus
- 22 • The Historical-Cultural Matrix of First-Century Palestine
- 23 • Pharisees and the Laws of Purity
- 25 • Jewish Law and Custom during the Time of Jesus
- 28 • The Cleansing of the Temple in Jerusalem
- 29 • "A Temple of the Spirit" — Beliefs of the Ancient Jewish Essene Sect
- 31 • What Do We Know about the Historical Jesus?
- 32 • Conflicting Birth Narratives and Archetypal Images
- 36 • Jesus' Childhood
- 37 • Jesus' Early Life and Socialization
- 40 • Jesus' Adolescent Years and Young Adulthood: Did He Travel to Asia?
- 41 • The Baptism of Jesus: Rebirth "from Water and Spirit"
- 46 • Jesus' Visions in the Wilderness and the Temptations Presented by Satan
- 48 • Parallels between Jesus and the Buddha
- 50 • Jesus' Miraculous "Deeds of Power"
- 51 • Jesus' Healings
- 53 • Jesus' Exorcism of Demonic Forces
- 54 • Jesus' Mastery over Matter
- 58 • Jesus' Mastery Over Death
- 60 • What are we to make of Jesus' "Mighty Deeds?"

- 62 • The Ethical and Religious Teachings of Jesus
- 63 • Jesus' Image of God and his Experience of God
- 65 • A God of Grace and Abundance: Birds in the Sky, Lilies in the Fields
- 67 • A God of Compassion: Father, Mother — or Both?
- 70 • Jesus' Image of God and the Influence of Gnostic Beliefs
- 72 • Christianity's Incorporation of the Feminine Aspect of God Found in Gnosticism's Idea of Sophia
- 74 • The Influence of Gnostic Conceptions of God as a Harmonious, Non- Gendered, "Whole"
- 75 • The Trinitarian God in Western Christianity — A Reflection of Patriarchy?
- 77 • Jesus' Experience of God: Intimate Knowing
- 79 • Conceptual Versions of the Christian God in the Middle Ages
- 80 • Jesus' Conception of God
- 83 • "Love One Another, As I Have Loved You"
- 89 • "Love your Enemies"… The Power of Forgiveness
- 94 • Jesus and the Self
- 98 • God's Kingdom Within
- 101 • Jesus' I AM Statements
- 105 • God's Kingdom on Earth — An Alternative Social Vision
- 109 • Gender Complementarity
- 113 • Communal Meals
- 114 • The "Kingdom of God" — in Heaven or on Earth?
- 119 • Reaching the "Kingdom of God"
- 123 • The Sacrifice of the Only Son of God
- 130 • Arrest and Crucifixion
- 134 • Risen from the Dead
- 140 • Jesus' Death — Substitutionary Atonement for our Sins?
- 140 • Introducing the Idea of Original Sin
- 143 • Additional Paths to Receiving God's Grace
- 144 • Connecting the Doctrines of Original Sin and Substitutionary Atonement

147 • For God So Loved the World...
152 • World Tree Symbolism, Cross, and Resurrection —
    A Cross-Cultural View
161 • Conclusion

165 • *Bibliography*
169 • *Glossary*
173 • *Footnotes*

Acknowledgments

Words are sometimes not enough to express our gratitude. The *One Truth, Many Paths* book series would not have been possible without the unwavering support of the following individuals: My editor Sari Friedman who believed in me and worked tirelessly, providing her invaluable input and insights; Patrick Miller who did all the formatting and design, and shared his impressive expertise on publishing and e-book production; Byron Belitsos who was instrumental with his guidance during the earlier stages of this project; my seasoned literary agent David Nelson who gave me a real chance; and all my friends and teachers who inspired me along the way. Last but not least, I would like to thank my beloved husband Rod Price for his patience and his steady support and encouragement, which kept me going through all the vicissitudes that were inevitably part of this journey.

Isabella Price

Introduction to the
Cross-Cultural Guides to Human Spirituality

LOUD voices have alleged incompatible differences between the Abrahamic traditions: Judaism, Christianity, and Islam. But must there be a clash of civilizations complete with a never-ending threat of terrorism, destruction, and violence? Must we continue insisting on differences of doctrine and ritual that lead to division, intolerance, discrimination, and conflict? Or can we choose to focus on beliefs and values held in common, paving the way for a more inclusive, cooperative, and peaceful world? I do not suggest that anyone deny or devalue his or her own religion — quite the contrary. I believe that a cross-cultural comparative perspective brings a deeper understanding of one's own favored tradition or practice. I experienced this phenomenon myself when my study of Buddhism opened the door for me to an in-depth understanding of Jesus Christ's original teachings.

The basic belief of religious pluralism is that there is truth in every spiritual tradition; and a similarly ethical framework which values compassion, humility, and charity. The interfaith orientation of this series recognizes that these ethical values are universal. Adherents of different religious denominations can coexist in mutual respect and equal dignity. These are also the ideals of the

Founding Fathers of the United States, and are represented by organizations such as the Parliament of World Religions. It is in this spirit of unity-within-diversity that I have written *One Truth, Many Paths*.

Integral Theory

I have researched the worlds' major religions, mythologies, and cultural histories using the new discipline of Integral philosophy. Integral theorists such as Ken Wilber have an all-inclusive view that acknowledges *all* of the wisdom traditions. Integral philosophy also incorporates modern scientific research from psychology, physics, and biology within its theoretical framework. Integral theory then applies contemporary evolutionary theory and the findings of developmental psychology to explain the unfolding of the different stages and structures in the development of human history, culture, and consciousness — including psycho-spiritual development. Integral philosophy offers a helpful perspective when analyzing the different perceptions of Jesus Christ or the evolving notions of the divine. For example, God, or Spirit, can be experienced in three primary and distinct ways:

1) God as Self or the "Great I" (first person or subjective);

2) God as the "Great Thou" or the "Holy Other" (second person or relational);

3) God as the "Great It," the Ground of Being or the Great Web of Life (third person or objective)

According to Wilber, all three ways, or "Faces of God," need to be embraced and integrated to bring about complete spiritual awakening.

Incorporating Myth into Integral Philosophy

Integral philosophy has made great strides in synthesizing modern science, evolutionary perspectives, and philosophical analysis of the world's wisdom traditions — but in his more recent work Ken Wilber ignores the significance of mythic themes and their impact on the modern and postmodern Western world. Integral theory locates mythology at the pre-modern stage of consciousness, where it is perceived as a historical-factual account. However, I believe that the symbolic-metaphoric dimensions of mythology can still offer inspiration to our modern and postmodern world. It is my conviction that mythic narratives are alive or dead, not true or wrong — but they need to be reinterpreted and updated. Myths have been a constant among all cultures throughout time and history. If revitalized, myths can still be relevant today.

Incorporating the Sacred Feminine

Interestingly, I noted that many classics on comparative religion exclude the idea of the Sacred Feminine, perhaps because they were primarily written by men. Books with an emphasis on Goddess symbolism and women's history have been written over the last few decades, usually from a predominantly feminist perspective; but, strangely, studies on comparative religion generally reduce mention of the Sacred Feminine to a few sentences. It is time to change this. To dismiss or denigrate an expression of the divine that can be traced back to the Paleolithic and Neolithic eras, and which continues to play an important role in practices such as the vibrant *Shakta*-tradition of India, is to tell only half of the story of our human experience.

In India, the Divine Mother represents the activating principle in the manifest world of matter. She is the indwelling divine, present in all being. In Jewish mysticism, the Holy Feminine — referred to as *Shekinah* — fulfills a similar function. Taoism's most famous symbols, the "yin" (feminine principle) and "yang" (masculine principle), are in constant interplay. Yin and yang are not considered rigid, incompatible polarities — rather they complement each other; together they form the universe. Historically, a rigid and exclusive gender hierarchy has been particularly apparent in the emergence of patriarchal structures and paradigms across cultures and religious traditions. As a result, a "harmonious balance" has been sacrificed. Today, more than ever, we need to regain balance for the sake of our survival as human species, and to restore the ecological balance of our planet and its equally precious other-than-human life forms.

The Three Pillars of *One Truth, Many Paths*

What is praised is one, so the praise is one too,
many jugs being poured
into a huge basin.
All religions, all the singing,
one song.
The differences are just illusion and vanity.
Sunlight looks slightly different
on this wall than it does on that wall
and a lot different on this other one, but
it is still one light . . . —Rumi

Saints and mystics across cultures and religions talk of a universal and inclusive God of love, compassion, and forgiveness. They view love as the basis of all reality and the force that drives evolution. Many mystics and saints have suggested that all life is sacred. They see us as one human family. They emphasize the interdependence and interrelatedness of all phenomena in the great cosmic web of Being. Indeed, representatives of all the major wisdom traditions have all taught the Golden Rule: "Do unto others as you would have them do unto you." The universality of ethical precepts—compassion being a core value—is just one aspect of our common spiritual heritage.

The *One Truth, Many Paths Series* focuses on three guiding principles found in every religious tradition, and which I call pillars:

1) Shared ethical systems and precepts
2) The esoteric-mystical core of each wisdom tradition
3) Universal symbols and archetypes present in religious myths of all traditions

Pillar One — Ethical Systems and Precepts

Ethical injunctions are an integral part of the scriptures and moral codes in all the wisdom traditions. For example, selfless service to the community is always considered an act of love and generosity that confers spiritual benefits. Ethical systems and precepts may have originated as a way of preventing social chaos and anarchy.

Pillar Two — The Esoteric-Mystical Core

The esoteric-mystical core in each wisdom tradition is another unifying principle. This core is sometimes referred to as "inner faith," an awareness of the divine within one's own being. Indeed, mystics of different faiths may feel more affinity for one another than they do for members of their own religions who emphasize only "external" aspects such as the proper way to conduct rituals, the adherence to particular dress codes, or the insistence on an exclusively literal-factual interpretation of scripture.

Pillar Three — Universal Symbols and Archetypes

The third pillar of commonality is that similar universal archetypes can be found in every religion. In this series, I focus on the following three major archetypes: The Mother, the Father, and the Savior-Hero. The idea of an archetype comes from the work of Swiss psychologist Carl Gustav Jung, who suggested that several basic archetypes or "patterns" can be found in our shared human "collective unconscious." Archetypes have shaped religious myths across cultures.

The Mother Archetype was celebrated in numerous ancient religious rituals as a sacred marriage between a goddess and a king. The worship of the archetypal "Great Mother" can be traced to the Paleolithic period more than 20,000 years ago. The Mother archetype represents the nurturing, healing, and life-giving powers; but can alternatively take on fiercer, destructive, terrifying forms — especially when associated with the phenomenon of death and dissolution. Examples of the Mother archetype include the Christian conception of Mother Mary, the *Shakta* conception of the goddess Kali in India, and the New Age conception of the Earth as Gaia.

The Father Archetype has been honored in many patriarchal societies and cultures ranging from the Abrahamic traditions to the mythology of classical Greece, where Zeus, the thunderbolt-brandishing "Sky God," was worshipped as "Father-Chief" of the Olympian pantheon of deities. As with the Mother archetype, the concept of God as a Father takes two modes. God can be viewed as all-merciful, compassionate, forgiving, and caring — a father who watches over "his" creation from "above." Or God can alternatively be seen as stern, angry, merciless, and punitive — a judge who rewards the "righteous" and punishes "evildoers." The idea of a vengeful Father-God has been used to justify acts of violence committed in "his" name against "unbelievers."

The Savior-Hero Archetype is encountered in all the wisdom traditions, and has inspired a rich legacy of mythic narratives recounting many great and wondrous deeds spanning the savior's early childhood to death — as, for example, in the well-documented life of Lord Krishna in India. In his classical study *The Hero with a Thousand Faces*, mythologist Joseph Campbell identified a universal pattern or structure that marks the journey of all savior-heroes: birth into the ordinary world; the call to adventure; a refusal of the call; meeting with a mentor and other helpers and allies; crossing the first threshold (tests, trials, and ordeals); a reward; resurrection; and the return to the community with the elixir of life. Savior-heroes earn lasting fame by performing great deeds and by instructing the members of their society in appropriate values and behavior patterns. Savior-heroes are willing to pay the ultimate price by sacrificing their own life on behalf of an ideal or a community.

Shared universal symbols are found as well, in particular that of the World Tree, Cosmic Tree, Tree of Life, also known as the *axis mundi* or world axis. These symbols and archetypes provide inspiration and facilitate our psycho-spiritual empowerment in this complex and ever-evolving, ever-unfolding universe.

Additional Dimensions

I emphasize our shared symbolic-mythological heritage and the universality of ethical-moral tenets, but acknowledge that religions are *not* all the same. I see them as equally valuable but different, and do not take a position on the legitimacy or veracity of *claims of superiority* or *uniqueness* in regard to religious figures, doctrine, and belief systems. In order to best understand each individual religion, we need to know the historical-cultural context in which it developed. We need to take external factors into consideration. These are factors that vary greatly from culture to culture. The same factors are subject to change as societies and cultures evolve.

I examine each religious tradition with respect. There is truth in every religion. It is my conviction that all religious paths can lead to salvation or liberation if the seeker has a profound, consistent practice. Spirituality, and the awareness of our own conscious Being, are integral to the human experience. The same fundamental questions are addressed by religious myths in every culture:

- Who are we?
- Where do we come from?

- How do we relate to this universe?
- Where do we go after we die?

One Truth, Many Paths

The approach of this series is to *simplify without oversimplification*. The material is organized so that complex subjects can become more easily accessible. Humans have come up with over four thousand different religions. This series aims to provide a concise, balanced, and in-depth introduction to the essence and fundamentals of the five major world religions: Hinduism, Buddhism, Judaism, Christianity, and Islam. Judaism, which has the fewest number of adherents of the five, is nevertheless essential because it is the foundational religion of the two other Abrahamic traditions: Christianity and Islam. Aspects of other wisdom traditions — such as Taoism, Confucianism, Shinto, Zoroastrianism, Jainism, Sikhism, and Baha'i—are interspersed, but included primarily within the context of and in comparison with the five major traditions. Also included (esp. in the upcoming publication, *In the Beginning: Creation Myths Across Cultures*) are discussions of *primal* or *tribal* traditions. Our destruction of the earth's ecological balance shows we must pay more attention to what the primal traditions have to teach us, not less.

Each *One Truth, Many Paths* publication provides an in-depth discussion of an aspect of human spirituality. Each subject area in this tapestry of the human quest to understand Spirit is discussed clearly, and with many examples, to ensure an accurate understanding. The scope of this series is ambitious, ranging from a discussion of ancient pre-modern beliefs to speculations on various New Thought movements and views of the Apocalypse and the Afterlife. I believe our human spirituality will evolve as we grow as individuals and collectively as a species, and I wish to be of service in this endeavor.

An Overview of My Journey

My research took me to sacred sites in India, Egypt, Israel, Turkey, Italy, Greece, Indonesia, Vietnam, Cambodia, Japan, the United States and other nations. I have put years into the study of spiritual and religious texts. My journey began with my horror over the events of 9/11, and finished with reverence for the human reaching for the divine — which takes many paths worldwide, but which, in essence, always seems to arrive at the same one simple truth. My goal has been to contribute to a deeper understanding between cultures and religions, in hope of a lasting global peace.

My professional experience includes the teaching of World History and Religion courses in academic institutions in Switzerland and California. I have studied Buddhism at the Buddha Gate Monastery in California, and repeatedly visited the ashram of Sri Mata Amritanandamayi Devi (known to millions of people worldwide as Amma, which means spiritual Mother, Mother of Compassion, Mother of Immortal Bliss). Amma is also called "The Hugging Saint." Her religion is "love."

I have participated in religious rituals across the spectrum of wisdom traditions, ranging from numerous Native American rituals in the Lakota tradition to Jewish Holy Day gatherings with Rabbi Michael Lerner's *Tikkun* community, which showed me that Judaism's love and generosity reaches across class, gender, racial, and religious divides. I have also participated in prayer practices with members of the Muslim community. All of these experiences across the spiritual traditions have been deeply emotionally moving to me. There are many of us, worldwide, who share the belief that there is an *equal amount of truth in all wisdom traditions*, and I hope to see this mutual respect and understanding grow. Thank you for being a part of this intellectual, metaphysical and spiritual journey.

How Christianity Fits into the Framework of *One Truth, Many Paths*

Our study of Christianity will include our three pillars of analysis: we will examine Christianity's ethical precepts, its esoteric-mystical core, and its cultural legacy of symbols and mythological themes. Our journey of exploration into the essence of Christianity will include discussion of the historical-cultural matrix of first-century Palestine and an examination of Jesus' birth, socialization, and adulthood using early source material. We will consider how Jesus' life fits into the classical archetypal pattern of the savior-hero's quest.

An Overview of Christianity within a Cross-Cultural Context

Jesus of Nazareth, the incarnation of God in Christianity, is one of history's most compelling, multi-faceted, and elusive figures. How was this charismatic first-century Jewish teacher recognized as "God incarnate?" First, he seemed divine to his followers during his lifetime. His apostles and disciples experienced him as extraordinary — many left their conventional lives and risked everything to follow him. They experienced a "presence of the sacred" while with him. Second, Jesus embodied the aspirations, dreams, and hopes of some of his Jewish contemporaries, leading them to view him as the prophesied Messiah. Third, Jesus' apostles and disciples experienced him as an ever-present divine reality after the event known as Pentecost, which occurred fifty days after his death.

Jesus' extraordinary significance for Christians is apparent in the testimony of his early followers who spoke of him in the most exalted terms imaginable. As the "Son of God," the "Word /Logos made flesh," Jesus embodies what can be seen and known of God in a perfect human life. As the "Living Water" and the "Bread of Life" he nourishes his followers. As the "Lamb of God" he constitutes the perfect sacrifice. Finally, as "the Way, the Truth, and the Life (John 14:6) and " the Light of the World" (John 8:12) he enlightens humans about the nature and will of God, and about the path to eternal life.

The presence of Jesus after the event of Pentecost is a central affirmation of early Christianity, of the Gospels, and of the New Testament. It is also the core message of Easter. This leads to a distinction made by biblical scholars, between the "pre-Easter

Jesus" and the "post-Easter Jesus" (this is a term from Marcus Borg, a preeminent biblical scholar and an influential voice in progressive Christianity). The "pre-Easter Jesus" is frequently referred to as the "Jesus of history." The "post-Easter Jesus" is called the "Christ of Faith." Biblical scholars point to the differences between the depiction of *Jesus before his death* and *what Jesus became after his death.* Whereas the pre-Easter Jesus was finite and mortal — though able to work extraordinary miracles — the post-Easter Jesus is a divine reality, God incarnate. The belief that Jesus had been both fully human and fully divine was implicit and widely felt in the centuries after his death, though not finalized and made an official doctrine until the fourth century CE. Most prominently, it was the Church Council of Nicaea — convened by the Emperor Constantine in 325 CE with the purpose of stopping the warring among Christian factions over the nature of Christ — that formulated this belief also known as the Nicene Creed.

The adoption of Christianity as the official religion of the Roman Empire by the Emperor Theodosius in the late fourth century CE led to additional changes and theological adjustments within the new faith. For example, the so-called fall/redemption theology — also known as the doctrine of atonement — gained increasing importance, especially in the Latin West, partly because it served the power needs of the imperial Church by reinforcing its role as mediator between God and humans. According to this doctrine, the entire human race was tainted by Adam's fall, and the death of an ordinary human could not possibly constitute an acceptable sacrifice. The Church now taught that God's grace could only be received by offering the sacrifice of a perfect human life. Thus, Christians came to believe that Jesus Christ suffered and died on the cross to *redeem the sins of humankind.*

Along with key passages from the Pauline letters, John's reassuring proclamation that "God so loved the world that he gave his only Son" provided the theological rationale for the doctrine of substitutionary atonement. This doctrine in particular emphasized the *uniqueness* and *exclusivity* of Jesus' sacrifice, suggesting that the inexhaustible reality of God had been manifest in just *one* perfect human being, who was then required to give his own life to atone for the transgressions of all.

This key passage from John doesn't have to be read within the context of the traditional fall/redemption theology. It could equally be interpreted as referring to Jesus' incarnation or his life as *a whole.* According to this progressive view, the divine manifested in the physical body of Jesus Christ so that humans might fully awaken to the divinity at the core of their own being by following this inspirational example. Such an understanding shifts the focus from a predominantly *static* hope of salvation in a presupposed *afterlife* to a more *dynamic* vision of the Christian life — a vision that involves a process of self-discovery, spiritual transformation, and active participation in *this* world.

Jesus' encounter with John the Baptist involved a baptismal ceremony that led to what we may call a grand epiphany. This apparent rebirth from "water and spirit," along with a purported supernatural event that included the audible voice of God, drove Jesus into the wilderness where he faced what biblical scholars refer to as the three "temptation narratives." Shortly after his baptism by John and this sojourn in the wild, Jesus began a public ministry that lasted between one and three years. At the beginning of his ministry, Jesus attracted a great following by curing the sick and — according to scriptural accounts — displaying his mastery over the laws of nature. Involvement in this miracle tradition gives dimension to the esoteric-mystical core of Jesus Christ's teachings as recorded by both the canonical and the non-canonical Gospels (in particular the so-called Gnostic scriptures). In my discussion I will focus on the following interconnected key themes: Jesus' image of God and his experience of God, love and forgiveness, Jesus and the Self, and Jesus' social vision of "God's Kingdom."

We'll learn how Jesus' God is a caring God of abundance who is described as an archetypal "Father" in the scriptures, and also, in metaphors, is reminiscent of the "Mother" archetype. The pre-Easter Jesus was a Jewish mystic who led a life that was fully centered in God. Jesus' God was *not* an article of belief, but an *experienced reality* that was illuminated in core teachings about unconditional love and the spiritual power of forgiveness. This was not the first time love and forgiveness have been taught in a wisdom tradition — but Jesus articulated these principles with a passion that has brought them to the forefront of human consciousness.

The process of going within and exploring our essential Christ nature is alluded to in the Gospels with many different metaphors that Jesus uses such as, for example, the image of the "mustard seed." However, we'll note how Jesus makes it clear that the process of self-discovery involves a long and arduous journey.

Finally, the focus will shift to Jesus' social vision — a vision that is commonly referred to as "God's Kingdom." But *what* was the content of this vision, and *how and when* would the Kingdom be established? Disagreement exists over the answers to these questions, but scholars agree that the Kingdom of God is a blessed state of affairs, a transformed world in which the last would be first and the first last. This vision of a Kingdom of God posed a threat to the Roman Empire, who had political control of Palestine during Jesus' lifetime. Jesus was led to his arrest and execution because of his vision of the Kingdom of God. He gave his life for it.

Those who followed Jesus and called themselves Christians changed history. Important tenets of the Christian faith and Church tradition include the multilayered doctrines of original sin, vicarious atonement, and redemption. Most prominently, this fall/redemption theology — promoted by the imperial Church — led to a new focus of the Christian life centered primarily on Jesus' passion and his death. I will discuss some essential aspects of the theological controversy that erupted around the problem of the "risen Christ." The resurrection of a savior figure is an archetypal theme found in many pre-Christian cultures as well (examples include the Egyptian savior-god Osiris, the Greek "god man" Dionysos (Roman Bacchus), the Persian solar deity Mithras, and the Aztec savior-hero Quetzalcoatl). The idea of resurrection will be discussed from a cross-cultural comparative perspective that addresses symbolic references such as the Christian cross and its possible connection to the universal World Tree.

Today, Christianity is the most widespread of all the great religions, with approximately two billion adherents. Nearly two thousand years of history have added an astonishing diversity to this religion, as apparent in its three major divisions: Roman Catholicism, Eastern Orthodoxy, and Protestantism. It would, however, exceed the scope of this book to discuss the history of the differences between these three divisions in ritual, doctrine, and scripture interpretation, and such issues are already well covered elsewhere. Instead, this volume will focus on today's progressive independent scholarship, exploring ideas that are considered factual and plausible by most biblical scholars, historians, and archeologists about the man known to history as Jesus of Nazareth. Jesus' teachings are discussed within the historical-cultural context of first-century Palestine, and, at the same time, are related to emergent concerns and trends in contemporary spirituality. I am *not* professing to speak for all Christians and Christianity. For the most part, my text reflects my personal interpretation as based on extensive research and scholarship.

The perception of Jesus Christ has undergone dramatic changes over the centuries. Today, as a result of the evolution of consciousness and culture, we seem to have as many diverse ideas about Jesus Christ and what he represents as there are colors in the rainbow — even among those who call themselves Christians and claim to follow his teachings. For example, if we follow the cultural stages outlined in Integral theory and Spiral Dynamics, then the ethnocentric "traditional Christ" proclaims in authoritarian fashion: "I am the one and only son of God. If you give yourself to me alone, you shall be saved and granted eternal life." In contrast to this, the "modernist Christ" is an embodiment of extraordinary human skills and a potential that can be strategically applied to achieve great success and abundance. A different conception, the world-centric "post-modernist Christ," would acknowledge that Jesus' teachings are one among many paths to the truth, and this path would emphasize egalitarian principles and universal compassion. Finally, to take it one step further, the "integral Christ" would affirm and celebrate the radical interconnectedness of all life. This last conception is similar to the cosmic Christ hinted at in Paul's writing, in whom all things are held together (and which is the sacred evolutionary impulse of Christ consciousness that drives the perpetual unfolding of the cosmos and all of life (human and other-than-human) in its multiple forms beyond all conceptions and limitations). Beyond the perception of the universe as an integrated whole, a follower of the "mystical Christ" knows the great diversity of life is an expression of the divine. The Christ of John's gospel, for example, reflects this mystical awareness when he encourages his disciples to realize their own Christ-like natures.

Those who live "in Christ" — to use a common Pauline term — reflect the level of Christ consciousness that integral theorists call "Integral Christianity" because they connect naturally with networks of people across nations and cultures who embody the non-dual mystical awareness of Christ.[1]

Early Sources of Information About the Historical Jesus

The four canonical Gospels of the New Testament (Mark, Matthew, Luke, and John) reveal the "historical Jesus." The term "canonical" means that these Gospels belong to the early Christian church's official "canon" of approved texts that comprise the New Testament — as distinguished from the non-canonical Gospels, such as the "Gospel of Thomas," that were left out. In our search for historical veracity, we analyze stories and quotes from both canonical and non-canonical Gospel sources.

Three of the canonical Gospels: Mark, Matthew, and Luke, are referred to as the Synoptic Gospels. This is because they share certain similarities: Both Matthew and Luke used the earliest-written Gospel, Mark, as one of their primary sources for the narrative of Jesus' public activity. The other source they likely used is referred to as the *Q source* (Q means "Quelle," the German word for "source"). Biblical scholars assume that material found in Matthew and Luke — but not in Mark — comes from this unknown additional Q source. The fourth Gospel of John is different in tone and content.

Of course, the New Testament contains more than four canonical Gospels. In addition to the Gospels, it is comprised of twenty-three documents written by Christians of the first century. Centuries after the life of Jesus many texts were approved and collected into the canon of scripture. By the fourth century, the New Testament consisted of the four Gospels about Jesus' life, teachings, and death; the Book of Acts that describes the activities of his apostles after his death; twenty-one epistles written to Christian churches and communities (thirteen of which are attributed to the Apostle Paul, known as the "Second Founder of Christianity" and the most prominent of the early Christians because of his missionary activities and his great theological contributions); and the Book of Revelation that describes John's vision of the cataclysmic end of the world.

Written in the last third of the first century — beginning with Mark, whose gospel was probably penned in the year 70 — the Gospels are, unfortunately, rife with discrepancies. All were written decades after Jesus' ministry and death by authors who had not themselves witnessed the events they discuss. Scholars mostly agree that all four canonical Gospels were originally written anonymously in Greek — not Hebrew or Aramaic, the chief languages of Jesus' day — by highly educated Greek-speaking Christians who lived decades after Jesus' death.

The earliest traditions about Jesus go back to eyewitnesses whose accounts were circulated by word of mouth for decades. These became the primary sources for the later Greek writers. But information based on oral transmission inevitably leads to modifications over time, depending on the subjective lens through which a particular storyteller experiences a certain event, along with embellishments along the way. This phenomenon accounts for some of the discrepancies. Scholars encounter distortions caused by the reliance on an oral tradition, and subsequent questions of authenticity, in the sacred scriptures of other wisdom traditions as well.

Bible scholar Bart Ehrman points out how obvious discrepancies in the Gospel narratives indicate that the oral accounts were being altered — and in some instances even created — to suit the occasions in which they were shared. By this he means that the needs, hopes, and convictions of the early Christian communities had to be addressed by the "evangelists" (i.e., the Greek term referring to heralds of the "good news"). In other words, as evangelists, the authors of the Gospels proclaimed the "good news" about Jesus *in* and *for their time and place* by "updating" or adjusting the story of Jesus for their own particular audience and context.

Because no central authority standardized the emergent Christian message, these varying Gospel accounts evolved into complex and multi-layered narratives containing combinations of imperfect memory, imagination, cultural biases, and direct testimony. They display multiple voices including the remembered voice of Jesus and the voices of early Christian communities testifying about what Jesus had become.

The quest for the historical Jesus is a huge enterprise that began in the period of European Enlightenment. The work started with discerning decisions about the timeline and the literal voice of Jesus. In recent decades, the so-called Jesus Seminar has focused on the historical Jesus, and formally votes on the historical accuracy of Jesus' sayings. Bible scholar Marcus Borg argues in his many books that the best approach is not to discard the later layers or voices of Christian communities as irrelevant, but rather to understand them for what they were: part of a rich, diverse, and evolving tradition reaching back to Jesus himself. The advanced work of the Jesus Seminar illumines the fact that the Gospels are clearly not "history books" nor "biographies" of the life of Jesus; they are not literal-factual accounts. Rather, they are a combination of metaphorical narrative, historical memory, and literary composition. The Gospels communicate through literary structure, plot, character development, themes, and symbolism. The New Testament influenced history and continues to inspire present-day readers as the most important book in the history of Western civilization — whether seen as a religious book of faith or as a cultural artifact.

The Historical-Cultural Matrix of First-Century Palestine

To truly understand Jesus and his teachings as recorded by the Gospels, we have to familiarize ourselves with the time, place, and culture in which Jesus lived. The region had suffered repeated violence: it had been conquered by the Greeks, Babylonians, and most recently by the Roman Empire. Individuals who opposed these conquerors met with torture and execution. Most of the population of this region belonged to one of the many sects of ancient Judaism, some of the better known sects were the Sadducees, Pharisees, Essenes, Samaritans, and Zealots. Christianity originally emerged as one of these many sects.

The population of first-century Palestine was responding to the political repression of the time and the unforgiving nature of Roman rule. Though the Roman Empire exerted oppressive political control and heavily taxed the Jewish populace, there was one area in which free expression was allowed, and this was regarding religious expression. Greco-Roman religions themselves were polytheistic, inclusive, and — in spiritual terms — tolerant: they did not emphasize the importance of one "correct doctrine" nor did they argue that the chasm between the gods and humans was unbridgeable.

Although Jesus probably spoke Aramaic, the Christian Gospels were written in Greek decades after Jesus was crucified, and they reflect Greek cultural norms and patterns of rhetoric. This Grecian view portrays a Jewish Messiah executed by the Roman authorities with approval from Jewish priests. The culture of the time was torn between Judaism and assimilation to Greek cultural norms and integration into the "larger world." Outside Palestine and in the less urban areas such as Nazareth, where Jesus' family lived, most people followed the Hebrew Bible known as the Torah. Their lifestyle involved regular attendance in the synagogue, the honoring of the Sabbath, and compliance with the laws of Moses, which stressed the worship of God (rather than of political rulers), and care for the poor. In the larger cities of Palestine, however, Jews were divided into sects that were more influenced by the dominant Greco-Roman political structure and culture. In fact, in the proximity of Nazareth was the town of Sepphoris, which was the provincial capital of Galilee during Jesus' childhood. Sepphoris was heavily influenced by Greco-Roman culture and even had a Roman theater, which seated about 3,000 spectators. Most scholars agree that it is more than likely that Jesus himself may have visited or even worked in this city.

Pharisees and the Laws of Purity

The Pharisees were passionately religious Jews who believed in conscientiously following the Hebrew Bible and the Mosaic Law. The first section of the Hebrew Bible, the *Torah*, features what is sometimes called the Five Books of Moses (Genesis,

Exodus, Leviticus, Numbers, Deuteronomy) because traditionally their authorship is ascribed to Moses. The Pharisees insisted that their income and produce be tithed according to scriptural mandate (given to orphans, widows, Levites and strangers), and they sought to live in a state of ritual purity. As householders, the Pharisees cultivated a sense of God's presence in even the smallest details of their daily life. They emphasized the sanctity of God and believed that Israel was called to be a holy nation in accordance with the Torah's holiness code.

The advantage of the Pharisaic approach to Jewish life was that it allowed the devout Jew to access God directly without engaging in the elaborate temple rituals that required the mediation of the Sadducees, the wealthy and aristocratic priestly elite. The Sadducees not only served as a liaison to the ruling Roman authorities, but also stressed the primacy of the Temple and the need to perform the sacrifices to God as prescribed in the Law.

In this context, the question arises: What was the relationship between the early Christians and the other Jewish sects, most prominently the Pharisees? The New Testament lists several of Jesus' disciples as Pharisees, including Paul, the great missionary of the early church. This fact suggests that considerable similarities existed between the teachings of Jesus and the major ethical tenets of the Pharisees. Moreover, the perception of the Pharisees varies considerably depending on the Gospel we may consult. The Gospel of Matthew, for example, portrays the "Scribes and the Pharisees" in a more critical light and has Jesus referring to them as "hypocrites" (Matt. 23:13-29). Yet, such statements need to be approached with utmost caution, biblical scholars agree. Karen Armstrong argues that the anti-Semitic tenor of Matthew's Gospel is rather a reflection of the tensions between Jews and Christians during the eighties of the first century CE when Christians were formally ejected from the synagogues because they refused to observe the Torah.

Other Gospels, such as the Gospel of Luke, paint a more favorable portrait of the Pharisees, showing Jesus arguing with them in an amicable manner. Jesus' teachings of loving-kindness and charity were mostly in accord with the basic tenets of Judaism, and are the same as those taught by the great Rabbi Hillel the Elder, which emphasize the primacy of compassion. Both Jesus and others in various ancient Jewish sects sought to renew and revitalize Judaism. Their endeavors have to be understood within the context of Judaism, which allows a relatively high degree of internal criticism. It cannot be emphasized enough that Jesus himself was deeply Jewish, even while he stood in sharp tension with some groups within Judaism at the same time. For example, Jesus' position differed from that of some who were in the priesthood and who followed a more rigorous interpretation of the laws of purity at the expense of compassion.

Jewish Law and Custom during the Time of Jesus

During Jesus' lifetime, there were massive pilgrimages to the large and relatively new temple in Jerusalem, which was known as the Second Temple (the First Temple had been destroyed in 586 BCE by the Babylonians.) The Second Temple was maintained by Jewish priests who were usually born into the ancient sect of the Sadducees (which no longer exists), and which were allied with the Greco-Roman political establishment and thus had more resources than other Jewish people.

Remaining pure was an important idea in the religious beliefs of this time, and one of the first things a pilgrim would do, before entering the Temple, was to engage in a purification ritual not unlike baptism: he or she would immerse in a spiritually cleansing water-filled bath known as a *mikveh*. The Sadducees who maintained the temple were subject to additional rituals and were required to adhere to strict levels of purity. Part of being "holy" meant keeping a distance from people and things that were considered impure. In fact the Temple itself was divided into parts based on these divisions. The outside part was called the Court of the Gentiles: this area was a marketplace for vendors who offered souvenirs, animals for sacrifice, food, and money-changing services. For practical reasons, sacrificial animals had to be purchased on site with a special "Temple currency" because Roman coins were stamped with the image of the emperor — who was believed to be divine by the Romans — and thus this money was unacceptable to the Jews who only worshiped God. Roman coinage had to be traded for "Temple currency" which did not bear the image of Caesar, and licensed moneychangers handled these exchanges. Further inside the Temple was an area called the Court of Women: this area was for Jewish women and men as well as those who could be unclean, such as those who worked with garbage, those who had been maimed, eunuchs, and lepers. This area was huge and multi-leveled, with porches and viewing galleries that looked down on the more restricted areas, so everyone could see what was happening below even if they couldn't be there in person. Further in was the Court of the Israelites, which could only be entered by men. The Court of the Priests, close to the center of the Temple, was for priests alone. The most sacred spot in the Temple was called the Holy of Holies: only the High Priest was allowed in here and he was only permitted to enter one time a year — on Yom Kippur, the Day of Atonement.

In contrast, Jesus stressed the importance of esoteric or "inner" purity over "external" purity, as evident in sayings such as his famous aphorism from the Sermon on the Mount: "Blessed are the pure in heart" (Matt. 5:8). Jesus also stressed the ethos of compassion, criticized the overly strict observance of the Sabbath, and challenged what he saw as an over-emphasis on tithing (i.e., taxes on agricultural produce). Tithing was related to the issue of purity since untithed produce was considered impure — but since the tithes went directly to the Temple treasury, Jesus pointed out that the Temple priesthood was compromised by economic and religious interests in upholding the purity system. Jesus criticized their system that, in his view, neglected justice: "But woe to you scribes and Pharisees! You pay tithes of mint and dill and cumin, but you have overlooked … justice, mercy, and good faith" (Matthew 23:23). The ancient sect of the Pharisees is no longer in existence, but at the time of Jesus they were what we'd call "blue collar" and working class.

The Cleansing of the Temple in Jerusalem

The Gospels of Matthew, Mark, John and Luke tell the story of Jesus implementing his own ideas of purity in his encounter with the money-changers — though they differ on the timing of when this cleansing took place. The Gospel of John describes this cleansing as occurring at the start of Jesus' ministry. The other three Gospels place this event in Jesus' final week on earth, following his triumphant entry into Jerusalem on what is now known as Palm Sunday.

In any case, the Temple was the focal point of worship and devotion for some, but not all, Jewish sects. A few Jewish sects, like the Essenes, avoided the Temple, communed directly with God, and lived in monastic communes in the desert. Still, Temple theology affirmed that this was God's dwelling place on earth, and Jews from around the world made the pilgrimage to Jerusalem to perform the animal sacrifices as prescribed by the Mosaic Law.

According to the Gospels of Mark and Matthew, when Jesus witnessed the exchange of money and selling of animals he was outraged by what he considered to be a desecration of the Temple. Jesus proceeded to overturn some of the moneychangers' tables and he drove the animal sellers out. Based on the accounts of the Gospels it is hard to know just how thorough Jesus was in this "cleansing of the Temple." It appears unlikely that he managed to shut down the entire operation, as biblical scholar Bart Ehrman opines. In addition, some of the details may have been exaggerated.

In the Gospel of Matthew, Jesus appears to be critical of the sacrificial practices of the Sadducees, who used animal sacrifice as a way to earn forgiveness for transgressions: "It is mercy I desire, not sacrifice" (Matthew 12:7). But as the Gospels suggest, another reason for Jesus' intervention was his disapproval of actions aimed at reaping financial benefits and profits in God's very sanctuary. Another reason may be found in Mark's prediction that the Temple itself would soon be destroyed. Ehrman argues that Jesus performed a symbolic act by overturning the tables, showing in a small way what was going to happen soon in a big way when the "Son of Man" (Jesus, in the guise of what scholars call a cosmic eschatological Messiah from heaven) would arrive in judgment. According to Ehrman, it is this additional aspect — also referred to as Jewish apocalypticism (a final war between good and evil) — that is essential for understanding the historical Jesus and his actions. We'll note later in more detail how Jewish apocalypticism was a popular form of belief held by some of the Pharisees and, in particular, by the Essenes. Apocalypticists perceived history and the evolutionary process itself primarily in dualistic terms, with two supreme forces contending with each other for control of the universe. According to this belief, the forces of good would eventually overthrow the forces of evil.

"A Temple of the Spirit" —
Beliefs of the Ancient Jewish Essene Sect

John the Baptist, a wandering ascetic and popular prophet whom Jesus encountered early in his ministry, expressed his apocalyptic worldview in unmistakable terms when he announced that God's judgment of a sinful world was at hand. John was a tireless and fiery preacher who urged the populace to repent for their sins. John also accused the priestly elite in Jerusalem of being hopelessly corrupt, challenging their claim to be "mediators" of God's forgiveness. Instead, John suggested repentance and baptism.

John the Baptist likely had ties to another major renewal group of first-century Palestine, the Essenes — he may have been a member of their community. The Essenes were very spiritual Jews who believed that the rest of the people of Israel had fallen away from God and had, therefore, become impure. To preserve their own purity apart from the corrupting influences of the world around them, the Essenes established their own monastic communities. One such community was located at a place called Qumran, the site of the discovery in 1947 of the famous Dead Sea Scrolls, an Essene library. The Dead Sea Scrolls are an expression of Jewish apocalyptic belief. The teachings of the Essenes, as revealed in these scrolls, stressed the importance of an esoteric "Temple of the Spirit" rather than an external stone temple. They referred to themselves as the "Holy Community." The Essenes departed from much of conventional Jewish practice. For example, instead of performing the old animal sacrifices, they purified themselves and sought forgiveness of sins by means of baptismal ceremonies, communal meals, celibacy, and the sharing of property. Many Essenes also dedicated years of their lives to ascetic practices of self-discipline, piety, and contemplation, some achieving astonishing powers of extrasensory perception not unlike the spiritual masters of India.

The Essenes, in common with other Jewish sects who were suffering under the harsh yoke of the Roman Empire, hoped for a savior who would deliver them from oppression and establish a society in which they could follow their spiritual practices without interference. Many of the Essenes' concerns were later shared by the early Christian communities. Yet what distinguished Jesus from the Essenes, who had completely withdrawn from society to prepare for Judgment Day, was his public ministry and his strong commitment to be *in* this world (but not *of* it) in order to spread his message of God's infinite love bent on universal salvation. Further, as a result of Paul's efforts, Christianity no longer had its original Jewish identity. Christianity grew in popularity throughout the world, partly as a result of extensive missionary efforts. Judaism remained a religion that gladly accepts converts but does not actively seek them.

What Do We Know about the Historical Jesus?

Scholars now agree that we know for a certainty very little about the historical Jesus. In fact, "the biographical details of Jesus' life are so meager that early in the twentieth century some investigators went so far as to suggest that he may never have lived,"[2] as Huston Smith notes. That possibility, however, was later rejected by most researchers. The first full-length account of Jesus' life is to be found in the Gospel of Mark that was written approximately forty years after his death (c. 70 CE). By that time, historical facts had been overlaid with mythical elements that were rather an expression of the significance of Jesus for the early Christian movement. As biblical scholars have repeatedly emphasized, the Gospels do not provide anything close to a full and coherent biography of Jesus.

Nativity by Edward Burne-Jones. Art in the public domain.

Conflicting Birth Narratives and Archetypal Images

But what, then, do we truly know of Jesus (or *Yeshua* in Aramaic)? He was born in Palestine near the end of the reign of Herod the Great, probably around 4 BCE. His parents were Jewish, and their names were Mary and Joseph. He may have been the firstborn, though this is not certain. He had four brothers and an unknown number of sisters, all presumably children of Mary and Joseph. However, church tradition later rejected the idea of Jesus having "biological" brothers and sisters because this possibility challenged the doctrine of the perpetual virginity of Mary.

Within the New Testament, the birth of Jesus is referred to only in two sources — the Gospels of Matthew and Luke, both written very likely in the last twenty years of the first century. Paul, the earliest New Testament author, whose genuine letters were written approximately between 48-64 CE, does not mention Jesus being born in any special way. Neither does Mark, the earliest Gospel, nor John, the latest of the canonical Gospels written likely near the end of the first century (90-95 CE). Moreover, the stories of Jesus' birth as found in Matthew and Luke give us two very different accounts.

According to Matthew, the family of Jesus lived in Bethlehem, and Jesus was born *at home*. Matthew tells of three wise men who follow a star, and are led to the newborn child. He also mentions the slaughter of male infants in Bethlehem ordered by King Herod the Great, which subsequently forces the family of Mary and Joseph to seek refuge in Egypt. After returning from Egypt, the family moves to Nazareth. Matthew emphasizes that the genealogy of Jesus goes back to Abraham, the great patriarch; from David onward his line is traced through the kings of Israel. Birth at Bethlehem and Davidic descent were criteria for making the case that Jesus was, in fact, the Messiah — the "King of the Jews" — in accordance with some Jewish beliefs, though there is no discussion of a possible Messiah in the Jewish Torah, which was written before Jesus' birth.

In Luke the genealogy of Jesus goes back all the way to Adam, and David's line is traced not through the kings, but through the prophets of Israel. Also in Luke, Jesus' family of origin starts in Nazareth, but must travel to Bethlehem to comply with the Roman census. Jesus is born during this journey, in *a stable*. After his birth the family returns to Nazareth. In Luke there is no mention of a star, nor of wise men; rather, we are told that shepherds gather around the newborn child. In another striking discrepancy, Luke doesn't write anything about the slaughter of infants and the flight into Egypt.

As one can easily see, the standard Christmas story represents an amalgam of the infancy accounts of both Matthew and Luke. Ultimately, the two accounts have little in common, except for the names of Jesus' parents and Jesus' birth in Bethlehem during the rule of Herod the Great. Otherwise, the two Gospels tell us completely different birth stories. While Matthew emphasizes Jesus' kingship, Luke traces Jesus' genealogy back through the Jewish prophets; Luke also has shepherds, who were marginalized people, come to greet the newborn child, which stresses Jesus' significance as a radical social prophet. By tracing Jesus' genealogy back to Adam, the father of humankind, Luke furthermore emphasizes Jesus' role as *universal savior* for both Jews and Gentiles. The discrepancies between these two Gospels are the basis upon which most reputable New Testament scholars have concluded that the nativity stories and genealogies of Jesus are not historical accounts but rather symbolic narratives created by the early Christian movement, which wanted to tie Jesus to Israel's Messianic tradition that began with King David.

Moreover, both Matthew and Luke powerfully express the ancient theme of light coming into the darkness — Matthew with the star shining as a messenger to the wise men, Luke with the glory of God appearing in the night sky as the angels sing to the shepherds. The use of light imagery reappears in John's Gospel where Jesus is called "Light of the World" (9:5).

The image of light, of course, is an archetypal theme found in basically all of the world's wisdom traditions. Buddhist legend, for example, tells us that all the worlds were flooded with light at the time of Buddha's birth (compare also to the term "en*light*enment" that is a metaphor of salvation, or liberation from suffering). The decision of the Christian church in the fourth century to celebrate Jesus' birth near the time of the Winter Solstice is another powerful expression of this light symbolism. Jesus, born at the time of deepest darkness, announces the coming of the light. In fact, Jesus *is* the light in the darkness.

The birth date of December 25, however, is not derived from any event in the Christian story. Instead, Christmas has pagan roots that trace back to the third-century Roman festival of the rebirth of the Invincible Sun ("Sol Invictus"), celebrated sometime around the Winter Solstice, the moment when the increased darkening ends and the lengthening of the daylight hours begins. And in the northern hemisphere, our pre-Christian ancestors filled their homes and meeting places with candles, decorated evergreen trees, rang bells, sang songs — all to call the sun back into the sky. Long before the celebration of the birth of the divine child, Jesus, the joy of new beginnings was celebrated by the birth of a luminous "holy child" — known by many names across ancient cultures — at the time of the Solstice. The magic of rebirth, light born out of darkness, is common to all people in northern regions. The name of this celebration of the young sun god's birth has come down to us as "Yule." The term means "Wheel of the Year" and refers to the endless cycle of changing light, temperature, precipitation, and foliage as manifest in the seasons.

Not surprisingly, the birth of Jesus Christ is hence celebrated around the time of the Winter Solstice. However, we find no evidence in the canonical Gospels that Jesus commanded anyone to celebrate his birth. Today Christmas has, unfortunately, become an expression of widespread commercialization that focuses primarily on personal gratification, excessive consumption, and gift exchange rather than on profound introspection and contemplation more attuned to the spirit of Jesus' message. We need to remember that the essence of the Christmas narrative is incarnation, the very idea that God has come into the world in the form of a human being known to the world as Jesus Christ. And his divine incarnation reminds us that, ultimately, our human nature is inherently divine and that we too have the potential of experiencing the mystery, the wonder, and the love of God in our own human bodies.

Jesus' Childhood

It is also worth noting non-canonical sources that contain stories of Jesus' childhood. One such source is the late second-century Infancy Gospel of Thomas (not to be confused with the sayings Gospel of Thomas). The Infancy Gospel of Thomas reports some remarkable episodes about Jesus as a boy. For example, around the age of five he makes sparrows out of clay on the Sabbath and, when criticized for breaking the Sabbath by working, claps his hands and makes them fly away.

What are we to make of such stories? Biblical scholar Marcus Borg writes: "These fanciful tales assigning extraordinary powers to the child Jesus are the products of early Christian imagination, in which the divine status of the post-Easter Jesus is uncritically projected back earlier and earlier into his life."[3]

This image of the "wondrous child" is another archetypal motif encountered in the mythology of many cultures. For example, the Greco-Roman hero Heracles slays serpents as a child. Buddha's birth legends include the story of thirty-two signs that appeared on his body and another story of how he walked seven steps into each of the directions after his birth, measuring out the entire universe, and then pointing towards heaven and earth. The Hindu tradition recalls Lord Krishna's many wondrous deeds as a child and adolescent: He defeats demons sent out to destroy him, and he reveals the entire universe in his mouth to his dumbstruck foster-mother.

Moreover, the massacre of innocent children by a tyrant king is a theme found not only in the Gospel of Matthew but also in the birth story of Moses whose life, together with all the other Hebrew infants, was threatened by the pharaoh. Similarly, the tales of Krishna's birth and childhood report the reign of the tyrant king Kansa, who issued an order that all newborn males had to be killed.

Jesus' Early Life and Socialization

While ancient birth stories must be approached with caution and regarded primarily as great metaphorical narratives combined with archetypal religious imagery, scholars agree that Jesus grew up in Nazareth in the hill country of southern Galilee about a hundred miles north of Jerusalem. Population estimates for Nazareth vary widely, from two hundred to two thousand people. Jesus' political and social environment appears to have been more cosmopolitan than one might typically imagine. For example, the Greco-Roman town of Sepphoris was only about an hours' walk from Nazareth. Trade from this region with other parts of the Mediterranean world was extensive. The area contained a considerable number of Gentiles, and the Greek language was widely used as a result of Hellenistic influences.

From a few hints in the Gospels and what we might assume about the socialization of a Jewish boy in first-century Galilee, a few conclusions can be drawn about Jesus' youth. First, it is likely that he went to school in the local synagogue in Nazareth where the emphasis would have been on reading and writing based on the Torah as the primary text. If Jesus' family was — as Bible scholars commonly assume — at least somewhat devout, Jesus would also have participated in the religious practices of Judaism. He would have learned the stories, prayers, and hymns of the Jewish tradition and celebrated the great Jewish holidays. It is reasonable to think that Jesus at least occasionally went on pilgrimage to Jerusalem to observe these festivals. Though we do not know much about daily and weekly religious practices at the time of Jesus, it is likely that he prayed the *Shema* twice daily, upon rising and going to bed. He no doubt observed the Sabbath, which included attending the synagogue for Torah study and prayer.

Once again we must emphasize that we have nothing close to a full biography here; the four Gospels contain too many gaps. The New Testament's only story of Jesus at the age of twelve recounts his visit to the Jerusalem Temple with his parents at Passover. The parents find him sitting in the Temple among the teachers, listening and asking questions, and even instructing them. When his parents scold him, Jesus replies: "Did you not know that I was bound to be in my Father's house?" (Luke 2:49) Luke concludes that after this event, Jesus "advanced in wisdom and in favor with God and men" (Luke 2:52). Since Luke's Jesus Christ is to be the universal savior for both Jews *and* Gentiles, it is not surprising that he offers a story that depicts the youth teaching the wise men in the Temple.

As to the social-economic context of Jesus' upbringing in first-century Galilee, we can certainly infer that he lived under a preindustrial agrarian domination system in which the rural inhabitants—roughly 90 percent of the entire population—consisted of peasants. Some peasants owned small parcels of land; others worked as tenant farmers or day laborers. This rural population included manual workers such as artisans, construction workers, fishermen, and low-ranking servants. We are told that Jesus eventually became a woodworker, following in the footsteps of his father Joseph who likely was a manual laborer. Yet being a carpenter did not necessarily imply an economic standing superior to the peasant class. In fact, a woodworker belonged to a family that usually had lost its land. With that said, however, we need to be aware that the search for the historical Jesus may be "in danger of becoming a quest for the historical Galilee."[4] Ultimately, whatever assumptions may be drawn from the context of first-century Galilee to argue a case for what kind of Galilean Jesus was, or wasn't, all these assumptions and inferences remain questionable and problematic at best.

Jesus' Adolescent Years and Young Adulthood: Did He Travel to Asia?

Little is known of Jesus' life after the incident in the Temple, until twenty years later when he appears on the banks of the Jordan to be baptized by John the Baptist. Because no reasonably solid biographical facts have emerged about Jesus' life during this interim, popular speculation speaks of Jesus having traveled extensively during these "missing years." Similarities between Jesus' original teachings and the essence of Asian wisdom traditions (predominantly Buddhism and the Vedantic tradition in India) have led some to believe that Jesus may have traveled to India. The case for Jesus' visit to India is primarily based on a manuscript from a Tibetan monastery that described a visit to Kashmir in northern India by a young man from the land of Israel. The man's name was "Issa" (very close to Isha or Yeshu, the Indian pronunciations of Jesus' name). According to the manuscript, Issa left home at the age of thirteen. He made his way along the well-traveled Silk Road to India where he spent twelve years studying with Hindu and Buddhist masters. By the time Issa completed the long trek back to Palestine, he was almost thirty. In addition to the purported Tibetan manuscript, which has been lost since the Chinese army invaded Tibet, local people in the area of Ladakh in the 1920's were well-acquainted with the enduring legend of "Saint Issa," whose name they said with great reverence. While the idea of a visit of Jesus to India is certainly understandable given the similarities of his esoteric-mystical teachings with core aspects of Hinduism and Buddhism, it needs to be emphasized that serious scholars reject this possibility due to the lack of convincing historical evidence. In fact, some of them even argue that the nineteenth-century legend of "Saint Issa" traveling to Asia is a hoax. Moreover, similar teachings do not necessarily suggest direct influence. Ultimately, the wisdom teachings of both Jesus Christ and the Buddha came from the very same Source.

The Baptism of Christ by Verrocchio & DaVinci.
Art in the public domain.

The Baptism of Jesus: Rebirth "from Water and Spirit"

At some point, Jesus embarked upon a spiritual quest that led him to John the Baptist. This dramatic encounter with John, who electrified the populace with his proclamation of God's coming judgment, is one of the most certain facts we know about Jesus. John had accused the priestly establishment in Jerusalem of being defiled and hopelessly corrupt, urging the people to repent and to accept the baptismal rite of purification in the Jordan River.

At the height of John's popularity, the Gospels suggest that Jesus in his late twenties, or around the age of thirty, made the long journey from Nazareth to Judaea to be baptized by John. Mark gives the following account:

> "As he (Jesus) was coming out of the water, he saw the heavens break open and the Spirit descend on him, like a dove. And a voice came from heaven: 'You are my beloved Son; in you I take delight'" (Mark 1: 10-11)

The parallel stories of Jesus' baptism in the synoptic Gospels all include a vision in which Jesus sees the spirit of God descending upon him accompanied by a voice that names him as God's beloved son. This is reminiscent of some of the prophets of ancient Israel who spoke of the divine spirit descending upon them: "The spirit of the Lord came upon me" (Ezek.11:5) and "The spirit of the Lord God is upon me" (Isa. 61:1).

As an element, water has always been a symbol of the archetypal Mother and the maternal principle. We emerged from the amniotic fluid of the water of our gestation. In the evolutionary process, all of creation was birthed out of water. About seventy percent of our bodies consist of fluids. Water is an agent for healing and sustenance. Without water, we would die. Water quenches our thirst and gives us life. Although water is commonly used for cleaning purposes, Jewish tradition held that "living water" is the only kind suitable for ritual purification, and to be "alive" water must be connected to a larger source such as the ocean or a stream. This may explain why John performed baptism rituals in the Jordan River — its living water was believed to possess energetic properties that stagnant water lacked.

On a symbolic-metaphorical level, this belief implied that the psyche was dead unless it maintained a constant connection with the deep streams of universal life. Jesus Christ alludes to this truth by promising the Samaritan woman "living water" that will be "a spring of water within ... welling up and bringing eternal life" (John 4:14). In another episode from John, Jesus meets a Pharisee, Nicodemus, to whom he says, "No one can enter the Kingdom of God without being born from water and spirit" (John 3:5).

The act of baptism is symbolically related to the archetypal theme of death and rebirth. Moreover, to immerse someone in water is to drown them symbolically. Immersion in the waters of baptism can thus be looked at as a form of death, as the Apostle Paul stressed in one of his letters to the Romans (6:3-4).

To conclude in Richard Smoley's words: "Like most rituals of the highest order, this symbolic death and rebirth has many meanings. To die and to be raised up from the waters of baptism evokes the death and resurrection of Christ ... Moreover, to emerge from the waters indicates a new birth, as one emerges from the waters of the (motherly) womb at the time of physical birth ... Since the waters symbolize the ground of materiality ... and the tides of good and evil that are the world, immersion in and rising from the waters also signify the journey of the soul ... Death to this world, symbolized by the rising from the waters of baptism, constitutes a new life in the spirit."[5] Ultimately, the act of baptism hence symbolizes death to our separate self, our ego, and rebirth into a new and more evolved stage of consciousness. As a result of his baptism by John, Jesus very likely underwent a profound internal transformation that soon led him to undertake the public ministry that he did.

Over time, baptism became a sacrament ("sacred secret") common to all Christian denominations. Practiced by religious traditions worldwide, baptism became also an integral part of the early Christian movement following the baptism of Jesus by John. Two forms of baptism are practiced: adult baptism and infant baptism. In some Christian traditions, adults are fully immersed in water upon their confession of faith that "Jesus Christ is Lord and Savior." This affirmation declares that they have become "born again." Other Christian traditions baptize infants by sprinkling drops of water on their foreheads. Most Christians view the baptismal rite as an external expression of an inner reality. Those baptized have been "cleansed of sin" by God, or "washed clean" by the sacrifice of Jesus Christ.

The story of Jesus' baptism also shows a rich appreciation of the Jewish scriptures and tradition. It commemorates the waters passed through by the Israelites on their way from bondage in Egypt to freedom and the fulfillment of God's promise. Similarly, the description of the opening of the heavens offers a powerful archetypal image. With the end of prophecy (there had been no great Jewish prophet since Malachi many centuries before) the heavens had seemingly been "closed," with God's voice no longer being heard. Now, however, the heavens were opening again with God's spirit descending like a dove. This type of opening affirms the divinity of Jesus' encounter.

Indeed, like other religious traditions, Judaism had many central figures who had visions of God and other "paranormal" experiences. Abraham and Jacob had visions of God, and Moses was a Spirit-filled mediator whose face glowed with the radiance of the divine presence he had experienced on Mount Sinai, the sacred mountain that symbolically connects the earthly plane to the higher worlds, another example of the *axis mundi*. Many of the prophets of pre-modern Israel heard the "call" and had visionary experiences of the sacred. Elijah, for example, was said to be experientially in touch with God's spirit. Other traditions' prophets have similar experiences, for example the Sioux chief Black Elk is reported to have journeyed in the Spirit.

Just like the prophet Ezekiel before him, Jesus now had a vision of the heavens opening to reveal a message from God. Ultimately, it was the experience of being baptized by John — according to Huston Smith "a testament to John's spiritual power"[6] — that drove Jesus into the wilderness for forty days. The forty days in the desert also evoke the number of years Israel spent in the Sinai wilderness and the forty days of the great flood in Genesis.

Temptations of Christ, 12th century mosaic at St. Mark's Basilica
Reproduction in the public domain.

Jesus' Visions in the Wilderness and the Temptations Presented by Satan

The vision Jesus experienced at his baptism was followed by a series of visions during his sojourn in the wilderness, an arid, sun-blasted area with cliffs, caves, and wild animals. There he undertook austere spiritual practices for purification purposes, including both fasting and praying. We are told that he was immersed in prayer and contemplation for hours at a time, sometimes all night. His visions in the wilderness are referred to by scholars as "the temptation narrative," "a vision quest," or "a wilderness ordeal"— depending on the perspective. Mythologist Joseph Campbell calls it the universally valid deed of the archetypal savior-hero.

Mark tells us that in the wilderness Jesus was "tempted by

Satan" (1:13). This occurs after a period of intense prayer and fasting, when Jesus was most likely in a non-ordinary state of consciousness. According to the Gospels, Satan appears to Jesus to confront him three times. The visions are nearly identical in Matthew (4:1-11) and Luke (4:1-13), though the sequence is different. The devil challenges Jesus with several conditional phrases such as, for example, "*If* you are the Son of God" — hence suggesting that Jesus would surely be able to take care of himself by using his power. First, Satan approaches Jesus after a lengthy period of fasting when he is famished. He invites Jesus to command the stones to become loaves of bread. But Jesus replies: "Man is not to live on bread alone, but on every word that comes from the mouth of God" (Matt. 4:3-4), which echoes a passage from the Torah (Deut. 8:3). In the second vision, the devil takes Jesus to Jerusalem and to the highest point of the Temple. There he says to Jesus, "*If* you are the Son of God, throw yourself down," thus suggesting that God and the angels would surely protect Jesus from harm. In this second temptation, the devil invites Jesus to perform a foolish act just to test his confidence in God coming to his rescue. Jesus responds: "You are not to put the Lord your God to the test" (Matt. 4:5-7). In the third "temptation narrative," the devil takes Jesus to a very high mountain where he shows him all the kingdoms of the world, all their riches and splendor. The devil offers unlimited power and control over everything, provided Jesus bows down and worships him. This is the ultimate temptation involving the rejection of loyalty to God. Jesus counters: "Out of my sight, Satan! Scripture says, 'you shall do homage to the Lord your

God and worship him alone'" (Matt. 4:10; see also Deut. 6:13). The Gospels inform us that after this third temptation the devil left and angels attended to Jesus' needs (Matt. 4:11).

These are the visions or temptations of Jesus Christ. They are still relevant in our modern and post-modern times when we witness unbridled materialism, greed for profits, excessive consumption, and ruthless aspirations for political hegemony. Yet, did these visions in the wilderness really occur as actual experiences of Jesus, or are they rather a creation of the early Christian movement? The answer remains elusive. It is literally impossible to make a probability judgment one way or another. Most scholars, however, regard it as historically highly likely that Jesus did spend an extended period of time in the wilderness soon after his baptism.

Parallels between Jesus and the Buddha

The three temptation narratives of the Christian tradition are reminiscent of the three temptations presented to Buddha, while he was sitting in meditation under his *bodhi* tree. The first involved lust and carnal desire, the second evoked the fear of death, and the third focused on the desire for political power and the lure of kingship. In the Buddhist scriptures, the tempter is *Mara*, lord of desire and death. What are we to make of stories such as these about temptations and the devil? Literal-minded Christians tend to think of Satan as hidden from sight, roaming in the astral realms. Yet, to think of Satan as "out there in some metaphysical realm," may be too simplistic. It ignores the deeper concept according to which the image of the devil also personifies forces *within* us that can be experienced in a very vivid, real, and personal manner.

The figure of *Mara* in Buddhism and the devil in the Judeo-Christian tradition both fulfill similar functions. They embody all of the worldly pleasures, aspirations, and attachments that hold us in bondage if we exclusively identify ourselves with them and indulge excessively in the temporary satisfactions they offer. The devil is also a powerful metaphor of the so-called shadow-self, which refers roughly to all that which is repressed or denied in our psyche. We have to first consciously acknowledge and re-own our shadow before we can release it. Only by re-owning it — a long and sometimes very painful process that is metaphorically also referred to as "journeying through the dark night of the soul" — can we prevent our shadow qualities from being fatally projected onto other people whom we perceive as our "enemies." Or, the shadow might be dissociated and projected into parts of our own psyche, perhaps showing up as a threatening monster in our dreams, comparable to the visions/temptations of Jesus Christ and Buddha. To consciously acknowledge our shadow is thus absolutely an indispensable part of the spiritual life.

Jesus' Miraculous "Deeds of Power"

Jesus Christ performed impressive "miracles" or "mighty deeds" during his public ministry. Because Jesus' miracles have received so much attention, they deserve a more extensive discussion. Though the details of miracles differ from Gospel to Gospel, these supernatural events can be categorized into four basic types: healings, exorcisms of demons, displays of mastery over matter, and the ability to bring people back to life after physical death.

Christ Healing Simon Peter's Mother, sketch by Rembrandt.
Art in the public domain

Jesus' Healings

Healings are the largest single group of miracles attested to in the Gospels; in them, Jesus is depicted as a remarkable healer. Jesus is said to have performed miraculous healings of the diseased or disabled, remediating ailments such as leprosy, blindness, deafness, fever, bleeding, paralysis, and other unspecified problems.

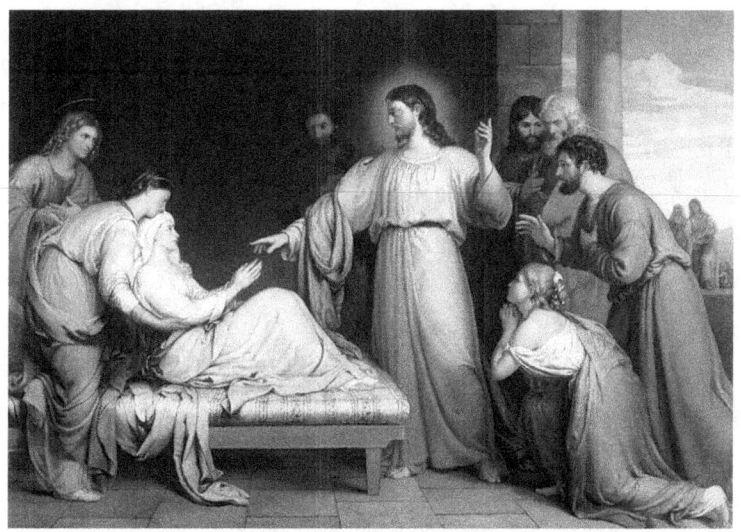

Christ Healing the Mother of Simon Peter by John Bridges.
Art in the public domain

In many of these stories, Jesus heals the afflicted person simply by pronouncing them cured, while in others he uses the same sorts of complicated rituals associated with other faith healers and charismatic wonder-workers in pre-modern Galilee. Other miracle workers were Haninah ben Dosa (first century CE), the ninth-century BCE prophets Elijah and Elisha, and

Honi the Circle-Drawer (first century BCE). Apollonius of Tyana, a famous Pythagorean teacher, miracle-worker, and healer in the Roman Empire during the first century CE — whose travel to India to meet the yogic masters and learn from their wisdom is well documented — is also said to have healed the sick, cast out demons, and even to have raised the dead in some instances. In fact, Philostratus' *Life of Apollonius of Tyana* exhibits a remarkable parallel to the "miracle-stories" in the canonical Gospels. For example, early in his ministry, Jesus heals a leper and instructs him not to reveal who has healed him. The leper disobeys, and Jesus' fame as a healer begins to spread throughout the area. In another episode, Jesus tells a paralytic in Capernaum to get up and walk, and the paralytic is then able to move. In another miracle scenario attested to only by Mark, Jesus heals a deaf-mute by touching the man's ears and his tongue with spittle, while he utters the words "be opened" (7:34). Mark furthermore tells the story of Jesus restoring sight to a blind man in the town of Bethsaida in Galilee by touching his eyes with spittle as well (8:22-26).

Jesus' healing act of restoring sight to people is related to the "blindness" metaphor frequently used in the Gospels. To be given one's sight, to see, means also seeing and following Jesus as "the way." In addition, this "seeing" relates to the "light and darkness" theme. John states explicitly that Jesus guides people from darkness to light just as he gives sight to the blind. John affirms that Jesus is the "Light of the World" (9:5); he brings *enlightenment* into this world just as the Buddha did five hundred years earlier. A famous Hindu prayer from the Upanishadic tradition in India states: "Lead us from untruth to truth, from *darkness* to *light* [author's emphasis], from death to immortality" (Isavasya Upanishad).

Generally speaking, one could say that the human condition is characterized by metaphorical blindness, by being "in the dark" — or what Buddhist tradition calls "ignorance." Most humans are disoriented and they often feel lost. The solution is to regain our sight, to have "our eyes opened," to come into the light so that we may be able to see again with the eyes of our hearts. Our spiritual masters guide us and make us "see" again, for it is futile to have the blind leading the blind: "Can a blind person guide another blind person? Will not both fall into the ditch?" (Luke 6:39 and Matt. 15:14). Words attributed to Jesus also refer to his healings in summary form. To messengers sent to him by John the Baptist he said, "go and tell John what you have seen and heard: the blind regain their sight, the lame walk, lepers are cleansed, the deaf hear, the dead are raised to life" (Matt. 11:4-5 and Luke 7:22).

Jesus' Exorcism of Demonic Forces

Exorcism, or driving out demons of people who have been possessed, is a common "miracle" attested to by the synoptic Gospels of Mark, Luke, and Matthew. Sometimes, the possessed suffer from additional afflictions such as muteness, that resolves once the demons are exorcised. In other instances, demonic possession manifests through bizarre and destructive behavior, reminiscent of mental illness. In Capernaum, Jesus meets a man "possessed by an unclean spirit" that "threw him into convulsions and left him" when Jesus commanded the spirit to "be silent" and to "come out" of the man's body (Mark 1:21-26). In the most elaborate and dramatic of the exorcism stories, Jesus meets a demoniac living in a graveyard. Naked, he howls day and night, bruises himself with stones, and with superhuman strength he breaks the chains with which he is shackled. Jesus expels the multiple demons from the man, and they enter a herd of two thousand pigs. The pigs then fall over a cliff into a lake and drown (Mark 5:1-20). This story is a powerful metaphor of impurity. The possessed man lives on the other side of the Sea of Galilee among "impure" tombs. Pigs — animals considered unclean in the religious traditions of the Near East — graze nearby. Under normal circumstances, impurity was seen as contagious. But in this particular story Jesus is not made impure by contagion; rather the re-verse happens. The unclean spirits are exorcised, the unclean animals destroyed, and the story ends with the possessed man restored to sanity. The powerful message is that the spirit of God present in Jesus overcomes impurity rather than being overcome by it.

The notion of "possession" by "evil spirits" is alien to the modern and post-modern Western worldview. It is, however, an integral aspect of tribal consciousness and is widely attested in indigenous cultures. Jesus' contemporaries, and pre-modern societies in general, took for granted that people could be possessed by spirits from other dimensions of reality.

Jesus' Mastery over Matter

Another set of miracles attested by the Gospels are those that involve Jesus' mastery over matter. A prominent event reported by the synoptic Gospels is the so-called Transfiguration. We are told that the inner core of Jesus' disciples experienced the presence of the sacred in him in a glorified form (Mark 9:2-4; Matt.17:1-8; Luke 9:28-36). On top of a mountain, traditionally identified as Mount Tabor in Galilee, Jesus begins to radiate light: His face "shone like the sun, and his clothes became a brilliant white." Moses and Elijah appear beside Jesus and the three have a conversation. The stories of the prophet Elijah, who after Moses is probably one of the most intriguing of the prophets of ancient Israel, are full of wonders and miraculous acts. According to the Jewish tradition (1 Kings,19:8) Elijah had a revelation of God on Mount Horeb (Horeb is another name for Mount Sinai, the "Mountain of God," where Moses received the Ten Commandments). Elijah's powerful personality and his magical death — an ascent to heaven in a fiery chariot — combined to accord Elijah a special role in Jewish tradition. In the Dead Sea Scrolls he appears as one of the forerunners of the Messiah. In the New Testament, many identified John the Baptist with Elijah (Luke 1:17; John 1:21). Some even thought Jesus to be Elijah (Matt 16:14; Mark 6:15); but Jesus rejected this, attributing the role of Elijah to John the Baptist (Matt 11:11-14; Mark 9:12ff).

Jesus, momentarily suffused with the radiant presence of God similar to Moses' "glowing face" at Sinai, must have made a profound impression on his disciples. In Mark, Peter was overcome and cried aloud. Then a cloud appeared, covering the mountaintop, and a voice said: "This is my beloved Son; listen to him" (Mark 9:7). Centuries later, when Greek Christians pondered the meaning of this vision, they concluded that the "powers" of God had shone through Jesus' transfigured humanity. Modern biblical scholars, of course, take a more critical approach. Marcus Borg argues that the Transfiguration is almost certainly a post-Easter metaphorical narrative. It affiliates Jesus with the two most famous prophets of ancient Israel. For a deeper understanding of the meaning of the Transfiguration, it is not relevant to debate whether this event really happened in a literal-factual sense.

In another display of mastery over matter attested by Matthew and Mark, Jesus walks on water to greet a boat with his disciples during a storm on the Sea of Galilee (Matt. 14:22-33). His disciples, distressed at the prospect of drowning, implore his help. Then they see Jesus walking on the sea; he commands the storm to cease and it does. In another famous incident at Cana, Jesus turns water into wine during a wedding, after the original supply of wine at the celebration runs out (John 2:1-11). Similarly, in what is known as the "Feeding of the Five Thousand," Jesus is able to provide food for a great number of people despite an initial lack of supplies (Mark 6:30-44; Matt. 14:14-21). The supplies on hand, just a few loaves and fishes, and Jesus' ability to multiply this miraculously, offers a powerful metaphor — namely, that God always provides for us what is needed, not only to the body, but ultimately for the soul as well. In fact, as we'll see, Jesus identifies *himself* as the "bread" that satisfies our hunger and our deepest yearnings for spiritual fulfillment.

The "Feeding of the Five Thousand" echoes the well-known story of ancient Israelites journeying through the wilderness being fed *manna* by God. While the reference is implicit in the synoptic Gospels, the connection to Israel in the Sinai desert becomes explicit in John, where Jesus says: "Our ancestors had *manna* to eat in the wilderness ... the bread that God gives comes down from heaven and brings life to the world" (6:31-33). When his disciples ask Jesus to give them bread always, he responds: "I am the bread of life. Whoever comes to me will never be hungry, and whoever believes in me will never be thirsty" (6:35).

Jesus continues to use this metaphor in his pronouncements at the Last Supper. In his last meal with his apostles on the Feast of Passover, the celebration of ancient Israel's liberation from Egypt, Jesus speaks of the bread and wine as his "body" and "blood," suggesting a "new" Passover ceremony (Matt. 26:17-29; Mark 14:12-25; Luke 22:7-22; John 13:1-30). The sacrifice of Jesus as "God's Lamb" — replacing the sacrificial lamb of Passover — provides salvation to the keepers of the "new covenant" and leads them to eternal life. This ceremony is re-enacted in Christian churches everywhere in the sacrament of the Eucharist. Jesus is said to be present wherever and whenever the ceremony of the Last Supper is celebrated. In the rite known to Roman Catholics as the Transubstantiation, the Holy Spirit miraculously transforms the substance of bread and wine into Jesus' actual "body" and "blood."

With that said, though, we should not forget that the roots of the Eucharist lie in meal rituals that were also an integral part of the Jewish tradition. The father or leader of the tribe would always bless the wine or drink, and the bread or food. Jesus, acting as the "rabbi" or teacher for his disciples, performed the very same meal ritual as an essential act of life. As the rabbi at the table, he exhorted his followers to perform future meal rituals in remembrance of him. Essentially, Jesus said that he would be present every time in the future when people gathered in his name would bless the bread and wine during a meal. The incarnation of Christ is hence expressed in both the sacramental principle of the Eucharist and, in a broader sense, in every mundane and simple meal if we call his presence into our awareness.

Jesus' Mastery Over Death

Finally, Jesus displays his mastery over death on four separate occasions. The raising of the daughter of Jairus from the dead is attested in all three synoptic Gospels. Jesus simply takes the hand of the dead girl and tells her to get up. Miraculously, the girl obeys (Mark 5:35-43; Matt. 9:23-26). A remarkably similar incident is attributed to another ancient spiritual master, Apollonius of Tyana, as recorded by his biographer Philostratus. Once Apollonius stopped a funeral procession and raised a young girl from the dead. Rumors erupted in the wake of this event that accused him of being a sorcerer with supernatural powers. Apollonius, however, explained that as a physician he had been able to recognize that the girl had been in a coma and that he had merely used his medical skills to revive her. Similarly, Jesus explained that Jairus' daughter had only been "sleeping" (Mark 5:39; Matt. 9:24). Other such stories, such as the raising of the widow of Nain's son, are only found in Luke (7:11-17), while the raising of the dead Lazarus, brother of Mary and Martha, is only mentioned in the Gospel of John (11). Lazarus has been dead for four days, when Jesus meets Martha and tells her: "Your brother will raise again" (John 11:23). Martha responds: "I know that he will raise again at the resurrection on the last day," (11:24) to which Jesus adds: "I am the resurrection and the life" (11:25) — this is one of the famous "I am" sayings found only in John. Jesus then proceeds to command the dead Lazarus to "come out" of his tomb, which he does to the utter amazement of everyone present. Lazarus is still bound with linen and cloth.

Just as John uses the story of the healing of the blind man as an occasion for Jesus to reaffirm "I am the light of the world," he tells us through the story of Lazarus that Jesus is indeed the resurrection and the life. In these passages, Jesus speaks of the resurrection as a present reality. The metaphorical meaning is that Jesus brings life to the dead just as he brings light and sight to the blind. As the resurrection and the life, Jesus calls people forth from their tombs, gives them life, and sets them free — not only on the "last day" but in the *here* and *now* already. Lazarus thus represents all human beings who are dead — in a literal and metaphorical sense — but will be restored to life by Jesus. The story of Lazarus can be equally regarded as John's post-Easter testimony to Jesus, reflecting at a minimum the experience of his early Christian community. Interestingly, the state of "nirvana" in Buddhism is also described in terms of "no birth" and "no death." Nirvana transcends the painful cycle of reoccurring birth, death, and rebirth. Similarly, the early Christian communities believed that Jesus would guide them from death to immortality and from darkness to light.

What are we to make of Jesus' "Mighty Deeds"?

A literal reading of these stories can result in a reader wondering if the stories are true. But narrowing the focus to *believing* or *not believing* that Jesus performed miracles leads to an "either-or" position in which the story's metaphorical meanings can get lost. Modern scholars generally accept that there is a historical core to the exorcisms and healings performed by Jesus, even though we may not be confident that any particular story provides an accurate report, especially given the discrepancies among the canonical Gospels. The first records of Jesus' public miracles were written thirty-five to sixty-five years after the events took place, and were written by people who relied on an oral tradition that had been passed down for decades.

As Christian missionaries spread out over the known world, the story of these miracles helped convince people to adopt the Christian faith. Many of these new converts shared beliefs found in the pre-modern world, which accepted the supremacy of spirit over matter without question. Jesus was viewed by some of his contemporaries, and some new Christians, as an exorcist and as a healer of diseases, and these abilities were attributed to the powers of Spirit working through him. In other terms, Jesus knew how to access the subtle energies that are always available to us, provided we understand how to work with these non-material dimensions of our being. Yet according to the modern scientific worldview, miracles are "impossible" because they violate the laws of Newtonian physics. A person can't walk on water any more than an iron bar can float on it.

Biblical scholar Bart Ehrman emphasizes that in the earliest stages of the Christian tradition, Jesus' followers came to believe that the Kingdom of God was already beginning to manifest because of these mighty deeds, and that "miracle stories" were to be interpreted in apocalyptic terms: "In the future kingdom there will be no forces of evil. Jesus overcomes evil now. There will be no demons; Jesus casts out demons now. There will be no disease; Jesus heals the sick now. There will be no natural disasters; Jesus calms the storms now. There will be no hunger; Jesus feeds the hungry now. There will be no death; Jesus raises the dead now."[7] Thus, the "mighty deeds" eventually offered a taste of what it was like, or what it would be like, to be in God's Kingdom.

Whether or not one interprets "miracle stories" as literal facts, they are powerful symbolic-metaphorical narratives. The narrative may be summarized as something like this: Israel has been possessed, paralyzed, blinded, deafened, silenced, crippled, and starved. Now it is to be restored to life again and made whole, sane, empowered, faithful, and nourished by God. Jesus is the fulfillment of ancient Israel's deepest yearnings and hopes.

These miracle stories — first told to help potential converts believe in the message and the person of Jesus Christ — serve a broader purpose as well. In Huston Smith's words: "What made Jesus outlive his time and place was the way he used the Spirit that coursed through him not just to heal individuals but, and this was his aspiration, to heal humanity, beginning with his own people."[8]

Jesus Teaches the People by the Sea by James Tissot.
Brooklyn Museum; art in the public domain.

The Ethical and Religious Teachings of Jesus

The public ministry of Jesus lasted between one and three years, depending on the Gospel we may consult, and began soon after the visions reported at his baptism and in the wilderness. The brevity of Jesus' public life is quite remarkable given his significance and his impact on history. Central figures of other religious traditions had much longer periods of public activity. The historical Buddha Sakyamuni taught for approximately fifty years after he attained Supreme Enlightenment, and the Prophet Muhammad carried out his mission for a quarter century after receiving revelations from Allah. In comparison, the mission of Jesus seems like a meteor flashing through the night sky.

While Mark's account of the teaching period in Galilee is

more or less evenly divided between Jesus' "miraculous deeds" and his teachings, it is interesting to note that Matthew and Luke both place a greater emphasis on Jesus' teachings.

Jesus taught primarily with parables (mostly short fictional narratives) and aphorisms (memorable short sayings). Some prominent examples of his parables are the stories of the "Prodigal Son" and the "Good Samaritan," while the "Beatitudes," a portion of the so-called Sermon on the Mount, represent some of the most famous aphorisms of Jesus. The aphorisms and the parables constitute the cornerstone of the tradition of the pre-Easter Jesus who was without any doubt a most gifted storyteller and a speaker of great one-liners.

Parables and aphorisms are a thought-provoking and interactive form of teaching. They are accessible to even to the most uneducated person. Jesus invited followers from every walk of life to shift their consciousness and to *see* things in a radically new way. This new way reflected a subversive and alternative form of wisdom that challenged the cultural norms and social conventions of first-century Palestine. Jesus' teachings are grouped primarily around the following four interconnected key themes:

- Jesus' Image of God and his Experience of God
- Love and Forgiveness
- Jesus and the Self
- God's Kingdom on Earth: A New Social Vision

Jesus' Image of God and his Experience of God

Jesus stands in the tradition of Jewish teachers and prophets for whom the divine was an experiential reality. In the pre-modern world of Jesus, the question was not whether God was real, the question was *what* was the experience of God *like*? And, when God was encountered, what did God *want* for and from Israel?

Experiences of God are omnipresent in the Jewish scriptures. Abraham had visions, heard the voice of God, and encountered heavenly visitors. His grandson Jacob, the father of the twelve tribes, had a vision of a ladder connecting this world to other dimensions of reality, and he saw angels ascending and descending on it. Genesis calls this ladder "the gateway to heaven" (28:17), that is, the doorway into another dimension of reality. Similar stories are told about Moses: he received his call to become Israel's liberator from a bush that burned without being consumed. At the end of Deuteronomy, we are told that Moses knew God "face to face" (34:10-12). Further, the books of the prophets abound with experiences of the sacred. The ninth-century BCE prophet Elijah experienced God in an epiphany on a mountain. Both Moses and Elijah, appeared next to Jesus and conversed with him during the so-called Transfiguration. Profound visions of God are also attributed to the prophets Ezekiel and Isaiah. Such experiences are reported to have continued well into the time of Jesus with charismatic Jewish healers and wonder-workers such as Honi the Circle-Drawer and Hanina ben Dosa. But what image of God did Jesus have and what was the nature of his experiential relationship to the divine?

A God of Grace and Abundance:
Birds in the Sky, Lilies in the Fields

In a strikingly beautiful image reported both in Matthew and Luke, Jesus invites his hearers to look at the world of nature as a disclosure of God's grace and generosity:

"This is why I tell you not to worry about food to keep you alive or clothes to cover your body. Life is more than food, the body more than clothes. Look at the birds in the sky: they do not sow and reap; they have no storehouse or barn; yet your heavenly Father feeds them. Are you not worth more than the birds? Can anxious thought add a single day to your life? ... Consider how the lilies grow in the fields; they do not work, they do not spin; yet I tell you, even Solomon in all his splendor was not attired like one of them. If that is how God clothes the grass, which is growing in the field today, and tomorrow is thrown on the stove, how much more will he clothe you! How little faith you have! Do not set your minds on what you are to eat or drink; do not be anxious. These are all things that occupy the minds of the Gentiles, but your Father knows that you need them. Set your minds on his kingdom, and the rest will come to you as well. So do not be anxious about tomorrow; tomorrow will look after itself. Each day has troubles enough of its own" (Luke 12:22-31; Matt. 6:25-34).

This teaching offered by Jesus in his Sermon on the Mount is so simple, yet revolutionary, that it overturns everything we have been conditioned to believe about existence. The idea is to let God, the source of all life, take care of everything. By looking at the birds and the lilies, we are invited to see God as life-giving, gracious, and generous. Jesus experienced reality as characterized by a cosmic abundance providing for all our basic necessities. We are to release our anxiety and worry, and to replace this with trust in God's generosity. According to Jesus, faith is trust in the generosity and grace of the divine.

Modern life, however, is complex. We often worry about commitments and demands that come at us from all sides. This constant worry keeps us in the future and in the past, projecting our concerns into a fictitious future or clinging to negative memories. Jesus invites us to live a life anchored in the present. When we free ourselves from all our struggling, we realize that nature does indeed provide everything. When we draw close(r) to the source of all there is, was, and will be…. all of creation becomes part of us. We become "clothed by divine glory," just like the lilies of the fields. Without trust, however, this glory is hidden from our sight. We feel that the world is separate from us and often hostile to our needs. Jesus offers an alternative vision of an earth filled with God's radiant presence that can free us from this limited perception. He also reminds us of the transient nature of all life by evoking the image of the grass growing in the fields *today* and being thrown into the stove *tomorrow*. Yet, the source of all life is gracious and generous. If we ask, we will be given. Every thought and request generates a response from the universe. Divine intelligence manifests whatever we can imagine, as the following quote from Matthew reveals:

> "Ask, and you will receive; seek, and you will find; knock, and the door will be opened to you. For

everyone who asks receives, those who seek find, and to those who knock, the door will be opened" (7:7-8)

In another analogy from nature, we read in Matthew: "God makes the sun rise on good and bad alike, and sends the rain on the innocent and the wicked" (5:45). The preconditions for all life — light and rain — are provided to the righteous and the unrighteous in equal abundance. The same principle applies to all of nature. An apple tree offers its fruits to everybody without judgment or discrimination. It is interesting to note that the image of a gracious, generous, and nonjudgmental God as evoked by Jesus counters the notion of a vindictive God who rewards the "righteous" and punishes "evildoers" — as expressed in the controversial Book of Revelation.

A God of Compassion: Father, Mother — or Both?

In the parable of the Prodigal Son (Luke 15:11-32), Jesus provides an image of God that evokes the archetype of a compassionate "Father" who yearns for this son's return from exile. When the father sees his son returning, he rises and runs to greet him. Then the father joyously welcomes his son and celebrates his homecoming, even though the son has squandered the money and support he previously received from his father. As a result of the Prodigal Son's loose living and carelessness, he spent much of his exile working as a swineherd, which violated the laws of the purity system and thus left him an "outcast." The parable demonstrates that "God is quicker to pour out his grace than man to take it in"[9] — to use the words of the great medieval mystic, Meister Eckhart. The father proclaims, "My son, you are always with me, and everything I have is yours" (Luke 15:31). This shows that neither dutiful obedience nor penitence and returning from exile are required to earn God's love. Instead, the love simply exists as divine grace. The Prodigal Son's older brother, who had obediently fulfilled his duties at home, became angry at the father's joyous welcoming of the less-responsible brother. Both brothers had to learn the truth about God's love. And both had to learn how to live together without grudges and resentments.

Marcus Borg reminds us that in Hebrew, the language of the Jewish Bible, and in Aramaic, which was the language Jesus probably spoke, the word "compassion" has rich metaphorical associations. It is the plural of a noun that in its singular form means "womb." Sometimes the association with womb is explicit: a woman feels compassion for the child of her womb (1 Kings 3:26); or, a man feels compassion for his brother, who comes from the same womb (Gen. 43:30). Also, within the context of its emotional connection with the womb, the term compassion is found in the following passage from Jeremiah, in which God appears to be the speaker and says:

> "Is Ephraim (Israel) my dear son? My darling child?
> For the more I speak of him, the more I do remember him.
> Therefore my womb trembles for him;
> I will truly show motherly compassion upon him."
> (Jer. 31:20)

God's "womb trembles," and God vows to show "motherly compassion" upon Israel. These are metaphors that express God as the archetypal "Mother."

In another example, Second Isaiah also portrays God as a mother with her suckling infant (49:15). In the light of the highly patriarchal culture of biblical Israel, this might be surprising at first. However, when it came to expressing its sense of the divine, pre-modern Israel also used imagery of divine motherhood associated with the origins of life. We can thus conclude that Jesus' statement "Be compassionate *as God is compassionate*" (Luke 6:36) is rooted in maternal imagery found in the Jewish tradition that portrays God as both father *and* mother. This maternal imagery is evocative that it embraces life-giving, nurturing, inclusive, and caring qualities. Like a divine Mother who generates her children from a cosmic womb, God gives birth to us, nurtures and sustains us. Just as a mother loves the children of her womb and cares for their wellbeing, so does God love us and care for us. Moreover, this image clearly questions the still predominant perception of God as an archetypal "Father" who is *separated* from "his" creation. It also challenges the notion of God as a punishing judge and enforcer of strict requirements.

The father in Jesus' parable of the Prodigal Son acts hence much more like a mother than like the patriarchs of the Hebrew Bible. When he sees his son, he runs out into the street, embraces and kisses him, flooding him with love. This is a father radiating the passionate compassion of a mother. Jesus' vision of God and the virtues that he celebrated — virtues arising from burning love, compassionate mercy, radical humility, and hunger for justice — are indeed an expression of God as the archetypal "Mother."

Jesus' Image of God and the Influence of Gnostic Beliefs

To fully understand Jesus' image of God, we need to examine perceptions of the divine found in the communities of Jesus' time. An important but little understood group of early Christians were known as the Gnostics — they basically believed that salvation of the soul from the imperfect and corrupted material world was attainable through a secret mystical knowledge referred to by the Greek word, *gnosis*. In the past, some scholars thought that Gnosticism predated Christianity and included some pagan religious beliefs and practices. Yet today Gnosticism is primarily defined in a Christian context. As a unique and recognizable belief system, Gnosticism is commonly considered to be a second century movement that influenced the subsequent development of Christianity. However, ultimately rejected as heretics by the mainstream orthodox Christian church, Gnostic Christians suffered the fate of having their core teachings condemned and their books largely destroyed. In 1945 some of their scriptures — including the complete text of the Gospel of Thomas — were rediscovered in the desert sands of Egypt. Today, these codices are collectively known as the Nag Hammadi Library. The most prominent of the Gnostic scriptures, the Gospel of Thomas, was likely written in the second century CE. However, its 114 short sayings attributed to Jesus are believed to be much older in content.

How did the Gnostics perceive God? And how was their

perception related to Jesus' image of God and to notions that evolved in the Christian communities shortly after Jesus' death? Elaine Pagels, an authority on Gnosticism, has convincingly demonstrated that some of the Gnostic sects looked at God as both father *and* mother. In her extensive analysis of different Gnostic scriptures, Pagels argues that many of these texts speak of a God who embraces both masculine and feminine characteristics. One group of Gnostics claimed to have received a secret teaching from Jesus through James and Mary Magdalene. Members of this group prayed to both the divine "Father" *and* the divine "Mother."

Referring to the first creation account in Genesis that states that humanity was created both male and female (1:27), some Gnostics concluded that the God in whose image we are made must consequently have both masculine and feminine characteristics. Others associated the archetypal divine Mother with the "mystical, eternal silence" and even with the "Holy Spirit."

Magdalen with the Smoking Flame, Georges de la Tour, c. 1640
Reproduction in the public domain.

Christianity's Incorporation of the Feminine Aspect of God Found in Gnosticism's Idea of Sophia

Some Gnostics used their Wisdom Literature to characterize the divine Mother as the essence of wisdom. In this context, the grammatically feminine Greek term for wisdom, *sophia*, is the equivalent of a grammatically feminine Hebrew term, *hokhmah*. In Jewish Wisdom literature, wisdom is sometimes personified in female form as the "Wisdom Woman," especially in the Book of Proverbs and in the Wisdom of Solomon. In Solomon, the divine qualities of Sophia, or wisdom, are more fully developed. She is the "fashioner of all things" and the "mother" of all that is good. Similar to God, she is present everywhere and pervades all things. She is omnipotent, and she is the sustaining source of all life. These are, of course, all attributes of God.

Marcus Borg argues that the term Sophia goes beyond the personification of wisdom in female form, but represents, in fact, the feminine aspect of *God*. Moreover, we find in the canonical Gospels several passages that associate Jesus with the figure of Sophia. In one verse, for example, Jesus speaks of himself as a "child of Sophia" (Luke 7:33-35; Matt.11:18-19). The likely connection here to Jesus' image of God as compassionate and "womblike" is remarkable. To say that God is like a womb is to say that God is a "Mother" as well, just as the personification of God as Sophia, or wisdom, suggests that God has a feminine aspect.

Yet, after the early period of Christianity, Sophia as a female personification of divine wisdom became an increasingly remote figure in the cultural tradition of the West. This was primarily a result of the teachings of some of the church fathers, most prominently St. Augustine (354-430 CE), who used hierarchical gender symbolism to argue that divine wisdom, although grammatically feminine and imaged as a woman in the Wisdom literature, is actually male. Thus, male wisdom became the true image of the divine, at least within the Western Church tradition. The image of Sophia maintained an underground existence in esoteric circles in the West and in the Eastern Orthodox churches, surfacing as the Sophiology movement in Russia in the last two centuries.

The Influence of Gnostic Conceptions of God as a Harmonious, Non-Gendered, "Whole"

While some Gnostic Christians prayed to God as both "Father" and "Mother," another group of Gnostics stressed that the divine is in reality neither male nor female but transcends gender polarity altogether. A third group of Gnostics suggested that the divine could be expressed in either masculine or feminine terms, depending on which aspect one intends to emphasize. For the most part, these diverse Gnostic groups agreed that the divine is to be understood in terms of a dynamic relationship of opposites that ultimately form a harmonious whole — similar to the two fundamental principles of *yin* and *yang* in Chinese Taoism. Judaism shared the conception of God as a single, whole, entity — though this entity was conceived as being without gender, form, or partition. Ironically, this concept of God as a harmonious, non-gendered "whole" was alien to orthodox sects within Christianity, Judaism, and other religions, who still use language to convey the impression that God is *exclusively masculine*. Indeed, the absence of feminine symbols and characteristics of the divine marks orthodox Judaism and Christianity (with the exception of the Virgin Mary in Roman Catholicism and again, the strong role of Mary and the image of Sophia in Eastern Orthodox theology). This relative lack of the role of the Divine Feminine puts Western Christianity in striking contrast to other religious traditions that emerged in ancient Egypt, Greece, Africa, Babylonia, Asia Minor (Turkey), among others. And in India, the Divine Mother, or Mahadevi, is still worshiped as another manifestation of the Supreme

Consciousness. She is considered fully on a par with male deities (although this has not yet translated into a weakening of patriarchal structures in India).

The Trinitarian God in Western Christianity — A Reflection of Patriarchy?

Many feminist scholars have argued that the long-held archetype of God as "Father" and "King" in orthodox Christianity, has subtly or overtly upheld a cultural pattern of male dominance. But how did this pattern originate in the West? With the emerging consolidation of the Church in the fourth century CE, the church councils hammered out the Orthodox theological definition of the Trinitarian God, a definition that increasingly reflected patriarchal structures. The imaging of "male" and "female" as archetypal expressions of the mind-over-body hierarchy was common among the church fathers. It is particularly evident in St. Augustine who believed that woman had been subordinate to man even in Eden. In his treatise on the Trinity, Augustine stated that woman in and of herself does *not* possess the image of God because she represents the body, the material, corruptible existence; whereas the male, symbolic of the hierarchy of mind over body, has been created in the image of God without regard to his relation to woman. In Augustine's teachings, we can see "the theological anthropology that makes the male the image of normative humanity and the woman the 'other' in the sense of the lower and incomplete,"[10] as noted feminist theologian Rosemary Radford Ruether puts it. Of the three divine persons, two — the Father and the Son — are described in masculine terms, but the third, the Holy Spirit, remains somewhat vague. The term Holy Spirit suggested, for example, the sexlessness of the Greek neuter term for spirit, *pneuma*. But in Latin the word for "spirit" is grammatically masculine (i.e., *spiritus*) — which makes the Trinity entirely male.

It is therefore important to reiterate that the exclusively male nature of the western Trinity is far from being consistent with the early Christian tradition. Rosemary Radford Ruether, in her monumental work *Goddesses and the Divine Feminine*, reminds us that in the Gospel of Hebrews the Holy Spirit is seen as "Christ's Mother" and also as the power that transports Jesus' to the mountain of his transfiguration. Moreover, during Jesus' baptism, the Holy Spirit descends on him in the likeness of a dove — a very ancient symbol related to the pre-Christian goddesses. Some of the Gnostics also spoke of the Holy Spirit in feminine terms, as the Divine Mother. Elaine Pagels points out that in the most prominent of the Gnostic scriptures, the Gospel of Thomas, Jesus contrasts his earthly parents, Mary and Joseph, with his divine Father (the "Father of Truth"), and with his divine Mother (the "Holy Spirit"). According to Pagels, other Gnostic sources equally suggest that the Holy Spirit constituted the maternal element of the original Christian concept of the Trinity that was later suppressed.

Unfortunately, all the sacred texts revered by the Gnostics and other early Christians were omitted from the canonical collection of the Church and branded as heretical by the orthodox Christians who prevailed. Gradually, all feminine expressions and imagery of God disappeared. The most notable exception has been the iconography of the Virgin Mary. In 431 CE, Mary was officially proclaimed *theotokos*, which means "god bearer." Many centuries later, her status was even more elevated when her Assumption became official doctrine of the Roman Catholic Church in 1950. Only four years later, she was officially proclaimed "Queen of Heaven" — a title that she shares with pre-Christian goddesses such as Inanna/Ishtar of Mesopotamia and Isis of Egypt. Mary, however, is excluded from the Holy Trinity according to official Church doctrine; she is thus *not* considered on a par with God the Father, the Son, and the Holy Spirit. Yet today Mary is venerated as the archetypal "Divine Mother" by many people, and many of her symbols are indeed reminiscent of pre-Christian goddesses. And her son, the Christ, clearly embodies both masculine *and* feminine qualities and characteristics. To put it into the words of contemporary mystic and poet Andrew Harvey: "Christ is as much a son of the Mother as of the Father, and his message is saturated with the deepest wisdom of the Sacred Feminine as well as with the truth of the Father. In his own life and teaching, Christ continues to offer the whole of humankind the most challenging possible example of what it is to live as a divinized sacred androgyne, a fully empowered child of the Father-Mother."[11]

Jesus' Experience of God: Intimate Knowing

The notion that the divine can be *experienced* is foreign to many people in the modern and post-modern world. The common concept of God is that of an anthropomorphic entity *separated from creation*. Because God is this "Super-Someone out there," the divine is perceived as a reality that cannot be experienced — with perhaps the exception of rare moments of "supernatural intervention."

In truth, of course, this perspective on God simply represents one aspect of divine reality. The image of a transcendent divine "Father" figure corresponds to what philosopher Ken Wilber calls the pre-modern "mythic God." The pejorative image of this mythic God is as an "old man with a white beard in the sky uttering dogmatic commands." Wilber says this image of God is an immature aspect of what he calls the "second-person" perspective on God as the "Holy Thou" or "Holy Other." Wilber reminds us of the dangers of getting *stuck* in *one* particular image of the divine. The "mythic God" of pre-modern traditional consciousness is a God that we can only *believe* in, not a God that we can truly know and experience. The term used for referring to God as separate from creation is *supernatural theism*.

As already established, the pre-modern "mythic God" is a God of *transcendence*, not a God of *immanence* indwelling in all of creation. Perhaps the most familiar example of this notion of a mythic "Father-God" of transcendence is the opening line of the Lord's Prayer: "Our Father in Heaven."

With that said, we should not forget that the Christian scriptures also speak of God's indwelling presence. Jesus himself said, "The kingdom of God is inside you" (Luke 17:21). The Apostle Paul expressed this idea succinctly in these words: "God is the one in whom we live and move and have our being" (Acts 17:28). Paul's statement affirms that we have our existence *within* God; Jesus states that God is in *us*. These concepts correspond to Wilber's first-person perspective on Spirit, that is, God as the "Great I" that is always present in the depths of our own Self, yet ever-abiding beyond the world of time and form. The divine is not "somewhere else" — rather, God is both all-encompassing as well as indwelling each of us, and is thus available in the "here" and "now."

Of course, this concept of a God of immanence has always been predominant in the mystical-esoteric traditions. Yet, most mystics do not perceive God as only present within creation, they argue that God is both immanent *and* transcendent, an understanding designated by theologians as *panentheism*. This term derives from the Greek words *pan* meaning "everything," *theos* meaning God, and *en* which is the Greek syllable for "in." Panentheism affirms that everything is *in* God, and also that God is *in* all things, even as it insists that God is ultimately *more* than everything.

Conceptual Versions of the Christian God in the Middle Ages

During the Middle Ages, the concept of a God *separate from creation* became the prevailing notion in the West. In its roots, the idea of a transcendent deity can be traced back to Greek philosophy and to early Christianity. After the twelfth century CE, Greek philosophy had a considerable influence on the church fathers, most prominently on distinguished theologian Thomas Aquinas (1225-74) who attempted to integrate Aristotle's arguments for the existence of a transcendent first cause based on reason with the Western Christian tradition. The European Enlightenment in the eighteenth century CE further supported the concept of an exclusively transcendent and depersonalized deity. Consistent with Aristotle's theory of an abstract and logically necessary "first cause" of the universe that could not intervene in human affairs or tamper with the natural laws, the Enlightenment laid the scientific foundations for the modern rationalistic worldview, emphasizing that objective material reality is the "only reality." Not surprisingly, the Enlightenment largely rejected religion as represented by the rigid doctrines and authoritarian structures of the Roman Catholic Church, in particular because of the Church's alliance with the ruling monarchies and its support for the horrors of the Inquisition.

The rejected "God of the Church" — or what Wilber refers to as the "mythic God" of pre-modern traditional consciousness — was now taken to be God altogether. As a result, the Enlightenment effectively removed the divine from the universe. Nature and the world became de-sacralized. The notion of God's immanence was replaced by the transcendent principle of the "prime mover," which is central to the naturalistic philosophy known as "deism." The problem was that not only was the "mythic God" of the Church rejected by modernist science in favor of a remote and impersonal principle, but, in addition, *other forms of spirituality and mysticism* were ridiculed and repressed as well. The validity of spirituality was denied, and spiritual expression was kept out of modernity.

Jesus' Conception of God

With this discussion in mind, let us now return to our examination of the nature of Jesus' relationship with God. It is important to note that the pre-Easter Jesus was not (yet) God but rather, God was the central reality of his life. Much is explained by Jesus' Jewish heritage. The Jewish experience is saturated with closeness to God, and the Jewish scriptures and practices mediated a life centered in Godliness. God was not simply an article of belief but an experienced reality for Jesus, who was what we may call a Jewish mystic. As a healer and exorcist, he felt the Spirit of God actively working through him. The visions he had at his baptism and in the wilderness provide ample evidence that God became an *experiential reality* for him.

Many of the narratives in the Gospels reveal that Jesus felt God's immanence and omnipresence. Jesus "knew" God. Jesus' language expresses an intimacy with God beyond cultural norms and conventions. Marcus Borg reminds us that Jesus used the Aramaic term *abba* to address God in prayer. The Gospel of Mark reports that Jesus used the term when he was praying alone in the Garden of Gethsemane before his arrest: "Abba, Father, all things are possible to you; take this cup from me. Yet not my will but yours" (14:36). Abba is an Aramaic term of endearment used by children to address their fathers, similar to the more intimate English words "papa" and "dahdah." Abba is also related to the Hebrew word for "father" (*av*). However, the Aramaic term implies a familial relationship and suggests that worshippers not carry the negative emotional baggage attached to a remote, stern, and punitive father-figure, but that rather they visualize God as a parent who lovingly and protectively holds his or her child. It should be admitted that Aramaic has no formal word for father. We may also note that it is Jewish custom to refer to

God as a father, although the Torah, written about five hundred years before the birth of Jesus, addresses God more commonly as "King" or "Lord." The term "Father" is used in the Christian Gospels to address God. It is not surprising that Jesus, who was male and lived in the highly patriarchal society of first-century Palestine, refers to God primarily as Father and/or as *abba*.

Jesus' experience of God as an intimate presence also included the feminine aspect of God, as discussed earlier. Jesus may have perceived himself as the "son of the Father/*abba*" *and* the "child of divine Wisdom/the Mother." The Mother-archetype may have been deliberately omitted or, perhaps, simply got lost in translation.

Ultimately, the divine transcends all gender designations. As Huston Smith rightly observes, we can conclude that, "Jesus would have found gender inappropriate in referring to God ... for God himself is *beyond* gender."[12] Beyond all human projections, hopes, and expectations, God is certainly no "father" in strictly anthropomorphic terms. Familial terms, however, were required in pre-modern Israel because family relationships were, and still are, intimate relationships that shape the human experience.

To conclude, Jesus modeled the viability of a dynamic personal relationship to a "Holy Other" that he called *abba*. Jesus' relationship to God reflects primarily what Wilber calls the "second-person" perspective on God. Jesus also taught others to pray to a personal God. Yet in contrast to the traditional "mythic God" of belief (a more un-evolved version of God in "second person"), Jesus' conception of the divine invites us to experience God and to actively engage in the process of inner transformation by surrendering our small conditioned self to the "Beloved Other."

"Love One Another, As I Have Loved You"

Love is the term most strongly linked with the teachings of Jesus, as is apparent in some of his most famous sayings:

> "This is my commandment: love one another, as I have loved you. There is no greater love than this, that someone should lay down his life for his friends."
> (John 15:12-13)

> "Love one another ... If there is this love among you, then everyone will know that you are my disciples." (John 13:34-35)

But what type of love is Jesus talking about in these passages from John? The love he refers to is different from what we might call "conditional" love. Jesus teaches pure and unconditional love. The Greek term for such love is *agape*. Agape does not want anything, and it does not do favors for the sake of having them returned. Other types of love are characterized by rules, projections, expectations, demands, and stipulations — involving reciprocity and narrow self-interest. It is no stretch to say that "love" is often understood as transactional, a form of bargain. We are conditioned by parents, society, cultural norms, and advertisements to believe that we are only "loved" *if* we do what we are expected to do, behave in a certain way, or have a particular physical appearance. If we break these norms and behavior patterns within the conventional framework of the "love of the marketplace," we get blamed because feelings are hurt and expectations are violated. Agape, however, does not engage in obligations and rules that we must follow in the world of convention. Moreover, it is not limited to the biological family but goes far beyond; family ties do not have a special status within the world of unconditional love. This helps to explain why Jesus is so willfully oblivious to family concerns and dismisses conventional family values altogether according to some passages in the Gospels: "Whoever does the will of God is my brother and sister and mother" (Mark 3:35). The same idea is expressed even more explicitly in the Gnostic Gospel of Thomas that records an incident in which Jesus turns away from his siblings and his mother. In the following passage from Thomas, Jesus advocates a radically new and countercultural approach to family life by saying, "my true brothers and sisters are those in spirit who do the will of God" (sayings 99 and 101).

Finally, one more distinction needs to be made. Unlike the many expressions of conditional and worldly love, agape does not necessarily imply a warm feeling toward another being. Because of the conscious and dispassionate nature of agape, this type of love is beyond all assessments of likes and dislikes. If agape is truly impartial, and if we are to bestow it on the just *and* on the unjust alike, then it must stand apart from our vacillating emotions and attitudes.

Unconditional love is possible only if we are free from worldly attachments and if we let go of our comfort and security needs. Similar to other wisdom traditions, esoteric-mystical Christianity emphasizes that this freedom from worldly attachments — referred to as liberation from suffering in Buddhism — is indispensable. Ultimately, this process also implies that we transcend our ego, our conditioned self-concept. In *Inner Christianity*, Richard Smoley suggests that the practice of unconditional love is the best path to liberation. He argues that agape has been known as long as humans have existed and that Christianity didn't discover this type of love. However, Smoley points out the uniqueness of the Christian path by arguing that it is Jesus' distinctive contribution to have made unconditional love the core principle of his teachings. While Jesus' great emphasis on agape undoubtedly stands in its own right as a distinctive contribution to the world, it should be noted that the "path of devotion" in Hinduism (also referred to as *bhakti yoga*) and other wisdom traditions advocate a similar approach.

The practice of devotion and selfless service — as it is found in the esoteric-mystical teachings of most wisdom traditions — continuously places us in a position of humility that allows us to rediscover the "childlike innocence" within that connects us to unconditional love and divine grace. Many of the sayings in the Gospels that are attributed to Jesus talk about the "innocence of children." Mark, for example, relates:

> "Let the little children come to me; do not try to stop them; for it is to such as these that the kingdom of God belongs.
>
> Truly I tell you: whoever does not accept the kingdom of God like a child will never enter it"
>
> (Mark 10:14-15)

In the Gospel of Thomas we read:

> Jesus saw some babies nursing. He said to his disciples, "These nursing babies are like those who enter the kingdom."
> The disciples said to him: "Then shall we enter the kingdom as babies?'
> Jesus said to them: "When you make the two into one, and when you make the inner like the outer and the outer like the inner, and the upper like the lower, and when you make male and female into a single one, so that the male will not be male nor the female be female, (...) then you will enter the kingdom." (22:1-7)

Unconditional love comes naturally and is spontaneous, just like the love of a child for his or her parents. Agape does not categorize or label persons and things; it is nonjudgmental and does not allow the kinds of prejudices that separate individuals, tribes, and nations from each other. By implication, everything we have learned and come to believe about conditional worldly love should be unlearned. Selfish love based on ego-gratification and personal needs cannot lead to divine grace.

At the core of Jesus' ethos and his message of unconditional love lies the *imitatio dei* — the imitation of God: "Be compassionate as God is compassionate" (Luke 6:36). For Jesus, love and compassion were not simply individual virtues; they convey his alternative vision of communal life, a sacred collective space, as embodied in the movement that came into existence around him. Compassion, commonly understood as profound empathy for the suffering of others, engages us in our totality — just as unconditional love does.

In his parable of the 'Good Samaritan' (Luke 10:29-37), Jesus sets an example for what could be called "compassion in action." Jesus tells the story of a man who was robbed, beaten, and left for dead on the road from Jerusalem to Jericho. A priest and a Levite both pass by on the other side of the road — they fear contamination from a corpse. A Samaritan — who, ironically, could be considered "impure" himself according to the purity system — stops, binds up the man's wounds, and pays for his care at an inn. The Gospel of Luke sets this story within the context of a dialogue between Jesus and a man who is an expert on the Jewish scriptures. The man asks Jesus what it takes to gain eternal life. Jesus responds by asking the man to summarize the Law to which the man replies:

"Love the Lord your God with all your heart, and with all your soul, and with all your strength, and with all your mind; and your neighbor as yourself" (Luke 10:27)

Jesus affirms the answer. The lawyer continues to ask, "And who is my neighbor?" After telling him the story of the Good Samaritan, Jesus asks the lawyer whom he considers to be the "neighbor" of the man who fell into the hands of robbers and was left on the road half-dead. The lawyer replies that it was the one who showed kindness. He is told by Jesus to leave and do likewise.

To "love one's neighbor as we love ourselves" refers to *all other human beings* we encounter in our lives. This includes people of whom we might be critical, or, worse yet, those whom we despise. In the currently existing climate of cultural polarization, this parable could be retold with different contemporary adaptations such as, for example, the "Parable of the Good Homosexual" could be presented to an audience of social conservatives, or the "Parable of the Good Republican" could go before an audience of Democrats. The unconditional love Jesus extolls is all-encompassing and can come as naturally as breathing. This type of love and compassion can transcend rifts and barriers — just as God's abundant grace causes "the sun to rise on good and bad alike" (Matthew 5:45).

On a deeper and more esoteric level, the commandment to "love our neighbor *as* we love ourselves" involves the realization that we are not separate from other human beings, we share something vital. Jesus commands us to love "our neighbor *as* ourselves" because, in essence, our neighbor is an extension of our very own being. It involves a complete seeing that your neighbor is you. There are not two separate individuals co-existing "out there," rather we humans (and all other-than-human life forms) are just different cells of the one great Chain of Being. Indeed, this is the good news exhorting us to show compassion for the suffering of others, even those who are far away, and to walk the demanding path of unconditional love that knows how to give and spend itself freely for the benefit of all beings.

Jesus is quoting the Torah when he commands his followers to "love your neighbor as yourself" (Lev 19:18) — a fact that has, unfortunately, all too often been omitted in the Christian tradition.

Finally, Jesus' most influential follower, Paul, also speaks of love as the primary Christian virtue. In his magnificent exposition in *First Letter to the Corinthians* (13), in which Paul seeks to provide guidance to the Corinthian Church, he highlights one of the most familiar verses in the New Testament: "There are three things that last forever: faith, hope, and love; and the greatest of the three is love" (1 Cor.13:13).

"Love your Enemies"… The Power of Forgiveness

The principle of unconditional love is related to another commandment in the Gospels that is one of the most misunderstood commandments attributed to Jesus, and one of the most challenging to put into practice:

> "You have heard that it was said, 'You shall love your neighbor and hate your enemy.' But I say to you: Love your enemies and pray for those who persecute you, so that you may be children of your heavenly Father." (Matthew 5:43-45)

> "But to you who are listening I say: Love your enemies; do good to those who hate you; bless those who curse you … If anyone hits you on the cheek, offer the other also." (Luke 6:27-29)

Jesus explains that it is easy to love those who love us, even "sinners" can do that. But how do we learn to love our enemies? At first, it appears impossible to put this commandment into practice. Moreover, why would we want to love our enemies? On closer examination, different perspectives and layers of interpretation can be applied to Jesus' teachings of forgiveness.

Often, the people we view as hostile are the ones who are mirroring our shortcomings, also known as our psychological "shadow." But if we become willing to take a honest look at ourselves, we may benefit and learn from the experience. In other instances, people who seem to be working against us and putting obstacles in our way can become our greatest teachers. They are the ones who — perhaps unwittingly — can facilitate our spiritual growth, provided that we dare to delve deeply. In this sense we need to be grateful to them, and gratitude is the first step toward "loving our enemies." Similarly, the Dalai Lama says that if we cultivate the right attitude, our enemies are our best spiritual teachers because their presence provides us with the opportunity to enhance and develop tolerance, patience and understanding.

The potential for healing and forgiveness is always available to us, even during hostile encounters. We can compare the workings of forgiveness to a homeopathic remedy that contains the poison necessary to facilitate the healing process. All the hatred and anger we may harbor against our "enemies" is the "poison" that already contains the seeds for release and forgiveness.

True forgiveness can only be applied toward those who have committed a hostile act against us. Yet in that act of true forgiveness lies a tremendously healing and liberating spiritual power. Jesus alludes to this power when he responds to the Apostle Peter's question, "Lord, how often am I to forgive my brother if he goes on wronging me? As many as seven times?" (Matt. 18:21) Jesus replies: "I do not say seven times but seventy times seven" (18:22). By responding in this way, Jesus is saying that we must forgive unconditionally and always.

The commandment to forgive is also emphasized in this line from the Lord's Prayer: "Forgive us our debts as we forgive our debtors." While this saying is usually taken merely as a high-minded sentiment, closer examination reveals how the practice of forgiveness can transmute negative emotions. If we carry anger, hatred, and enmity in our hearts toward other people, no matter what they have done to us, we will experience the toxic effects ourselves. More suffering and destruction will ensue. We will reap what we sow; this is the basic law of causality. But if we truly forgive, we will be forgiven in turn. In other terms, we will be acquitted of our shortcomings to the exact degree to which we acquit others of theirs.

Forgiveness offers an escape from the monstrous and perpetual cycle of hatred and revenge that, at times, appears to be the driving force in this world. The practice of forgiveness is a steadfast refusal to see wrongs, or, if seen, a refusal to keep them alive by holding on to them. Moreover, forgiveness is the ultimate act of generosity, since it gives without keeping count; and it is the ultimate act of freedom, since it liberates us from bondage to potential harm or loss. By refusing to care about any presupposed damage we proclaim our detachment and immunity to the damage, and thus we can "turn the other cheek."

This is true forgiveness, the forgiveness Jesus talked about; but while forgiveness is often praised, it is rarely practiced.

People may believe that the act of forgiving implies that they have to overlook genuine wrongs and to sacrifice justice and fairness. Viewed in this context, forgiving may be perceived as a sign of weakness. On closer examination, though, we can see forgiving as an act of strength. The human ego, our conditioned self-concept, wants to exonerate itself at all costs. We frequently blame others for all sorts of errors, and minimize our own shortcomings while exaggerating those of others. Jesus asked: "Why do you look at the speck in your brother's eye, with never a thought for the plank in your own?" (Luke 6:41) Here Jesus commands us to be nonjudgmental. Ultimately, true forgiveness is only possible from a place of nonjudgment, courage, and inner strength.

Finally the question arises: Whom are we forgiving? The most obvious answer is that we are forgiving other people. Yet all the wisdom traditions teach us that other people are, in essence, the same as us. People may have different physical appearances, and they display unique talents and distinctive behavior patterns. Obviously, each one of us has his or her special gift to give to the world. Yet, while our contributions to the world are distinctively unique, as humans we share the same desires, hopes, and vulnerabilities. To forgive others thus also means that we forgive ourselves. By inviting people to love others as they love themselves, Jesus expresses the imperative to show compassion toward others *and* toward ourselves. Indeed, if we are to see reality as it is — beyond all of our egotistic distortions — we can recognize our shared participation in the one, single, undivided source of all being. Jesus sees this one true sacred essence, which is steady and life-giving as the sun and the rain. By connecting with this essence in unconditional love and forgiveness, we can rise to the higher stages of consciousness and spontaneous, natural love that Jesus extols, and we can know true love.

The instructions to "love God with all your heart" and "love your neighbor as yourself" are not exclusive to Jesus' teachings and Christianity. The same message is at the core of the countless sacred texts, including those central to Buddhism, Judaism, Hinduism, Jainism, Islam, Confucianism, and other traditions.

But Richard Smoley emphasizes that it is Jesus' unique contribution to the spiritual life of humanity to have given the idea of forgiveness so much attention. In an act of ultimate forgiveness, at his most dire moment while dying on the cross, Jesus utters the following words according to Luke: "Father, forgive them; they do not know what they are doing" (23:34). The centrality of forgiveness in Jesus' teachings offers a way out of the perpetual cycle of revenge and retaliation and leads to inner peace.

Jesus admonishes his followers that "anything you failed to do for the least of my brothers, you failed to do for me" (Matt. 25:45). He commands them to love one another "just as I have loved you" (John 13:34). Divine love is unearned and freely given. It transcends any relationship based on conditions, comfort, and expectations. God cannot relate any differently to one person than to another, and even an enemy is deserving of God's unconditional love. Even though the "human love of the marketplace" depends mostly upon the degree of satisfaction we experience in relationships, we do have the potential to love in an unconditional way. The message taught by Jesus is that true and authentic love will lead to a fundamental transformation that changes our entire being and brings joy into our hearts.

Jesus personified the radical and life-changing nature of unconditional love. This type of love will make peace even with those who are hostile toward us. Moreover, it will invite divine grace back into our own existence. In the end, Jesus' teachings can only be effective when we *become* the teaching ourselves.

Jesus and the Self

Jesus devoted many of his teachings to the subject of the "self," or what is commonly referred to as the "I" or "me." Most humans identify themselves by describing their ego-centered self, which can be considered a disguise as it gives an illusory sense of identity by investing itself with social status, titles, material possessions, physical appearances, likes and dislikes, nationality, race, religion, party affiliation, and so forth. Moreover, this conditioned self creates the erroneous belief that we are separate and apart from everything else in the universe. Ultimately, this "I," or illusory self, is the most fundamental cause of human suffering, as the Buddha taught more than two thousand years ago. We find a similar teaching in the Christian contemplative tradition. Father Thomas Keating, who is considered by many to be one of the few genuinely realized Christian saints in today's world, writes in *Intimacy with God*: "The (false) self developed in our own likeness rather than in the likeness of God, is the self-image developed to cope with the emotional trauma of early childhood. It seeks happiness in satisfying the instinctual needs of survival/security, affection/esteem, and power/control, and bases its self-worth on cultural or group identification."[13]

The other component of the "I" is our true Self, our essential nature. This is the mysterious stillness and space within us that is always present. Our essential nature is immutable, infinite, ever-abiding beyond the world of time and form, birth and death. Through all the changing states of mind and emotions, our true Self remains the steady observer, the great non-dual witness of our activity and inactivity. Utterly unaffected by activities of the body and mind, this witnessing awareness operates similar to a movie screen that displays burning buildings and raging floods without ever being burned or drowned. This underlying awareness within *is* the core essence of our existence; it is what Ken Wilber refers to as the "First Person or Face of God," the "Great I," the non-dual witness within that connects us to Spirit. Sometimes this true Self is also called the "I AM" or the "I AM presence." Buddhism refers to it as our inherent *Buddha nature*, and in the Vedantic tradition of India it is the *Maha-Atman*. This concept is well established in the world's esoteric-mystical traditions.

Even though Jesus didn't specifically use the terms "conditioned self" or "ego identity," he alludes to the illusory sense of self in some passages of the canonical Gospels. Luke, for example, tells a story of two men going up to the temple to pray. One is a Pharisee, the other a tax collector. The Pharisee is praising his weekly fasting and displays his pride at his prompt payments of tithes on all purchased produce. He thanks God for not being greedy and dishonest like other people, such as thieves, adulterers, and tax collectors. However, the tax collector, standing far off, is beating his chest, crying out: "God, have mercy on me, a sinner!" Luke concludes with the following words attributed to Jesus: "It was this man (the tax collector), I tell you, who went home acquitted of his sins. For everyone who exalts himself will be humbled; and whoever humbles himself will be exalted" (Luke 18:10-14).

This parable is aimed at those who feel sure of their own righteousness while arrogantly looking down on everybody else. It also relates to Jesus' teachings of the "last being first, and the first being last." When the ego dominates — as it is the case with the Pharisee's self-righteous attitude — the focus is on the small "I", on "me" and "mine," not on a higher awareness. This attitude leads inevitably to judgment and thus to separation from others. Yet the divine can be found only in a state of non-dual realization without judgment. The first step to reducing judgment is to develop enough humility to recognize the self-righteous self-importance with which the ego likes to invest itself.

A rich variety of metaphors in the Gospels allude to the true Self, our essential nature. One example is the "seed" of which Jesus speaks in a parable found in Matthew (13:3-8). Some of the seeds fall by the wayside and perish because they can't take roots, others are eaten by birds, and a few fall on fertile soil where they produce an abundant crop. In those examples, the "seed" is a metaphor for the spark of the divine within us. The truth has been planted in each one of us, and it grows just like a plant until the day of the harvest, or God-realization. The path, however, requires patience and perseverance similar to the nature of the seed that grows slowly and invisibly. Another of Jesus' metaphors for the true Self is light. In Matthew we read: "You are the light of the world ... When a lamp is lit, it is not placed under a basket, but on a lampstand, where it gives light to everyone in the house. Like the lamp, let your light glow among your fellow humans, so that, when they see your good works, they may give praise to your Father" (Matt. 5:14-16). The light metaphor is even more emphasized in the Gnostic Gospel of Thomas where Jesus tells his disciples that they "come from the light" and that they are "children of the light, the chosen of the living Father" (saying 50). Gnostic Christians often referred to the true Self as a "spark," and God as the divine light from which the spark emanated. Gnostics commonly believed that individual sparks of divine light had broken off from God and were trapped within the human body. In our ignorance, most of us humans are unaware that this spark of light exists within us. Yet when we become aware of our true nature, the Self, we merge back into the divine light. The "light" metaphor in Christian scriptures also beautifully evokes the historical Buddha's urging to "be a lamp unto yourself."

In another passage from John (3:8), Jesus compares the workings of the Spirit to the wind, saying, "You hear its sound, but you do not know where it comes from or where it is going." In other words, Spirit works in unpredictable ways. The evidence of its existence is indeed subtle, and comparable to a faint breeze that goes unnoticed. This equation of Spirit with breath or wind is found across many cultures. The Navaho Indians, for example, talk of the "Holy Wind" that refers to the air, breath, life force and essence of Spirit that suffuses creation.

Ultimately, our true Self is to be found deep in our hearts. The Self, or "Great I," is eternal and unchanging. It is a treasure that is not subject to the same kinds of worries and concerns about material possessions that come from our ego-centered self. The true Self can neither be destroyed nor stolen because it *is* the core essence of who we are. However, it is buried under layers upon layers of mind-constructed beliefs, conditioned patterns, and habits. To discover its existence, we have to delve deeply. Today, some researchers use the term "heart intelligence." One of the quintessential scientific discoveries about the heart is that it plays a significant role in our awareness. At the Institute of HeartMath, scientists have found compelling evidence that the heart communicates with the brain and the body by way of both an extensive neural network and an electromagnetic field interaction. The heart's magnetic field is about five thousand times stronger than the brain's. In the light of this most recent scientific research it is interesting to note that the heart — rather than the brain — was considered the seat of memory, intellect, conscience, and emotions in ancient Egypt.

God's Kingdom Within

Statements in the canonical Gospels and in the Gnostic Gospel of Thomas make explicit references to "God's Kingdom" which can be found *"within us"* (Luke 17:21). We also noted this phrase earlier, in connection with Jesus' teaching regarding God's indwelling presence. In *Putting on the Mind of Christ*, former Catholic monk and modern mystic Jim Marion reminds us of Paul's injunction in Philippians 2:5: "Let the same mind be in you that was in Christ Jesus." Yet, how do we "put on the mind of Christ" and see through his eyes? These words call on us to go *beyond* the conditioned mind of our small ego-self that sees the world in terms of polarized opposites, and to move instead into the "larger and all-inclusive mind" of Jesus Christ. Religion is not just about believing in the creedal statements or admiring Jesus, but about acquiring his consciousness. God's Kingdom is hence not primarily a "geographical place" where we may go when we die, but rather refers to an awakening into a new dimension of being and relating to the world in the *here* and *now*. In this context, the "Kingdom" symbolizes a state of transformed consciousness. Jim Marion paints a portrait of Jesus as a master of non-dual awareness — way ahead of his time and the level of understanding of most of his contemporaries — calling people to a radical transformation of consciousness based on deep spiritual practice. Similarly, the living Jesus of the Gnostic scriptures emphasizes *gnosis*, self-knowledge and self-discovery, to a greater extent than does the Jesus of the New Testament. Self-knowledge is ultimately knowledge of the divine. The Gnostic Jesus speaks of "illusion" and "ignorance," not of "repentance" and "sin" as in the canonical Gospels. In *The Wisdom Jesus*, Episcopal priest and teacher Cynthia Bourgeault reminds us that the Greek term *metanoia*, commonly translated as "repentance," literally means "to go beyond the small mind" into the "large mind" of Jesus. Instead of being our "savior," the Jesus of the Gnostic scriptures comes as a wisdom guide who opens the door to a deeper spiritual understanding.

When the disciple attains liberation, Jesus no longer serves as spiritual master. The two have become equal, as the following saying attributed to Jesus states in the Gospel of Thomas: "I am not your teacher ... Whoever drinks from my mouth will become like me; I myself shall become that person, and the hidden things will be revealed to that person" (13 and 108). Here Jesus adds a shockingly intimate reciprocity to the act of teaching. This is not a hierarchical relationship between teacher and disciple, but rather a process of profound inter-being: I in you, you in me, all in God, God in all. This saying alludes to the path of self-emptying love (*kenosis* in Greek) modeled by Jesus who "humbled himself to be born in human likeness, obedient even to the point of death on the cross" (Philippians 2:8-9). Jesus always responded with the same motion of self-emptying, of *descent* to a lower place. The process of continuously renewed giving and receiving is where God ultimately dwells. Cynthia Bourgeault reminds us that the way of *kenosis* — the free and radical squandering of one's entire life force — is the revolutionary path that Jesus introduced into the collective consciousness of the West.

The Gnostic Jesus is thus portrayed as a spiritual guide, a teacher of wisdom — not unlike the Buddha, as Elaine Pagels emphasizes. The differences between the "Gnostic Jesus" and the "Christ of Faith" of the emerging Church tradition are thus considerable, to say the least.

Orthodox Christianity as represented by the imperial Church argued that a chasm separates humanity from its creator, and that Jesus is the "Son of God" in a *unique* way, forever distinct from the rest of humanity whom he came to save. The more esoteric notion that self-knowledge is knowledge of God — the

"Kingdom of God within" — is still largely absent from mainstream Christianity, with some important exceptions such as, for example, the mystical side of Eastern Orthodoxy, Quaker spirituality, and Integral Christianity, which draws from the contemplative Christian tradition. Self-knowledge also challenges the "mediator position" of religious institutions that claim to offer the *one* and *only* path to salvation. If the divine can be accessed directly and found in the depths of our own Self, then the usefulness of a cardinal or bishop may be questioned. To use an analogy, it would be like trying to sell air to breathe when air is all around and freely available.

In contrast to the "Christ of Faith" of the Church tradition, the Jesus of the Gnostic scriptures is closer to the approach of Hinduism and Buddhism, both religions of self-realization. The Gnostic Jesus also evokes the Greek philosophic tradition: "Know yourself" was the fundamental principle of the oracle at Delphi. The same approach can be found in the mysteries of ancient Egypt, where the importance of self-discovery and self-knowledge was equally stressed to the initiates. Finally, it should be noted that the Apostle Paul himself also alluded to the awakening of this "hidden wisdom" in his *First Letter to the Corinthians* (2:7), as the Gnostics liked to stress.

Jesus' I AM Statements

Any discussion of "Jesus and the Self" would be incomplete without including a few of Jesus' famous "I AM" statements. These statements are recorded in the Gospel of John: "I am the way, the truth, and the life" (14:6); "I am the door" (10:9);

"I am the light of the world" (9:5), and so forth. What are we to make of these sayings? Viewed from the perspective of esoteric-mystical Christianity, these utterances constitute extremely powerful statements about the relation of the small self to the greater "I" that is the true Christ. For example, "I am the door" is to be understood not just as an exclusive claim made by the God-Man Jesus, but also as an affirmation that our "I AM" nature, the divine essential presence within, is the door through which we may all eventually enter into a state of non-dual awareness — Jesus Christ merely points the way. "I am the way, the truth, and the life; no one comes to the Father except by me" (John 14:6) is *not* a narrow sectarian claim but a mystical utterance of the truth that the ineffable mystery of the divine cannot be encountered except through what we may, in this context, refer to as the "inner Christ," or our "Christ consciousness."

Viewed in this light, these "I AM" utterances no longer seem exclusive. Rather, they remind us that by penetrating to the core essence of our being we can access the consciousness at the heart of the universe. Additional evidence can be found in Jesus' statement: "In very truth I tell you, before Abraham was born, I am" (John 8:58). The esoteric-mystical Christ speaks through the God-Man we call Jesus and declares his existence as having predated Abraham. This statement — which deliberately uses the present tense "I am" instead of "I was" or "I existed" — does not refer to a previous incarnation of Jesus Christ. Rather, it alludes to a state of non-dual Christ consciousness beyond time and history, where there is no past or future…. but only the eternal now.

The journey to the core of our being is long and arduous. In the Gnostic Gospel of Thomas, Jesus tells us: "Seek and do not stop seeking until you find. When you find, you will be troubled. When you are troubled, you will marvel and rule over all" (saying 2). The emphasis here is on seeking rather than finding. The journey into the core of who we truly are is indeed disturbing because, as we discover our inner light, we will also discover the psychological "shadow" of our ego-centered self. Yet if we are willing to face our "inner darkness" the ensuing turmoil will be transmuted by the light, and we will be initiated into God's kingdom. This will indeed be our second birth as "new and divine human beings."

Mystics in all traditions tell us that we have "to die before we die." This refers to the death of the ego, our separate self, which has to occur before we can experience our "second birth of water and spirit" as symbolized by Jesus' baptism. This "rebirth" opens the door to the "Kingdom of God." Spirit works in unpredictable ways. Often, insight is a slow and gradual process. Patience and persistence are pivotal. The process of self-discovery requires that we master our thoughts and emotions.

Entering the Kingdom of God is very difficult and commonly comes after intense inner turmoil: the "wailing and grinding of teeth" (Matt. 24:51) will be inevitable, as noted. The Gospel of Matthew makes clear that, "narrow is the gate and constricted the road that leads to life, and those who find them are few" (7:14), and, "many are invited, but few are chosen" (22:14). Most people live in a state of ordinary conventional consciousness; they do not really know who they are. In another passage in Matthew,

Jesus invites some of his disciples to follow him and to leave it to "the dead to bury their dead" (8:22). This is a reference to the "walking dead"—those who are spiritually unconscious or asleep and have not yet awakened to the truth. The Gospel of Thomas is even more explicit. Here Jesus declares: "I took my stand in the midst of the world, and in flesh I appeared to them. I found them all drunk, and I did not find any of them thirsty. My soul ached for the human children, because they are blind in their hearts and do not see…" (28). The Gnostics acknowledged that pursuing "gnosis", or self-knowledge, engages each individual in a solitary, difficult process, as one struggles against strong internal resistance. They characterized this resistance to "gnosis" as the desire to sleep or to be "drunk", that is, to remain unconscious or ignorant. Countless forces oppose us, distract us, beguile us, so that we lose track of whom we really are and where we have come from. Whoever remains "blind," ignorant, and oblivious to the truth, cannot experience spiritual fulfillment. What is therefore most needed is insight. As we have already established, what distinguishes the Gnostics from Orthodox Christians is that they insisted that it was not sin, but rather ignorance, that involved a person in suffering. As is in Hindu and Buddhist belief, the Christian Gnostics stressed that the fundamental problem in life is human ignorance, forgetfulness, and lack of insight. In another passage in Thomas, Jesus admonishes his followers: "If you bring forth what is within you, what you have will save you. If you do not have that within you, what you do not have within you will kill you" (70). Again, the emphasis here is on our psycho-spiritual evolution and the bringing into manifestation of the divine spark of consciousness at the core of our being. If we fail to do so, it is not just a failure to live up to our fullest potential but that which remains unrealized actually turns on us and destroys us from within. The human soul bears within itself the potential for liberation *and* destruction. It is up to us to make a free and conscious choice.

God's Kingdom on Earth — An Alternative Social Vision

Matthew has Jesus define his mission in the first and greatest of the five discourses he artfully constructs. In the famous Sermon on the Mount, Jesus declares that he has not come to abolish the Jewish Law but rather to fulfill it (5:17). For Luke, on the other hand, the mission of Jesus is proclaimed in his first sermon in the Nazareth synagogue, on a text from Isaiah (61:1-3):

> "The spirit of the Lord is upon me
> because he has anointed me;
> he has sent me to announce
> good news to the poor,
> to proclaim release for prisoners
> and recovery of sight for the blind;
> to let the broken victims go free,
> to proclaim the year of the Lord's favor"
> (Luke 4:18-19)

Luke uses Jesus' first sermon to make clear that Jesus is fulfilling the prophecy of Isaiah, and that Jesus is the prophesied Messiah anointed with the Holy Spirit who has come to proclaim the good news to the poor. This proclamation appealed to the masses of a peasant population who suffered from brutal political oppression, and tithes and taxation imposed to pay onerous Roman tributes and to support both King Herod's ambitious building projects and a large bureaucracy living in opulence in the Temple in Jerusalem.

In the "Sermon on the Plain" (6:20-49), a series of memorable short aphorisms, Luke reports that Jesus blesses and consoles the poor, hungry, those who weep, and those who are hated and suffered discrimination. Jesus declares that they are the ones who will inherit the Kingdom of God. Luke follows this series of blessings with a set of woes starting with: "But woe to you who are rich, for you have had your time of happiness" (6:24). Far from seeing wealth as a blessing from God for having lived wisely and having observed God's commandments, Jesus saw it as a preoccupation with possessions and as idolatry: "You cannot serve God and money" (Luke 16:13; see also Matt. 6:24). And, even more explicitly, in the Gospel of Mark: "It is easier for a camel to pass through the eye of a needle than for a rich man to enter the Kingdom of God" (Mark 10:25).

Jesus renounces all material possessions, and is a wandering, itinerant teacher. Luke's Jesus is poor and dependent on the hospitality of others. Similarly, his disciples must go out in poverty to teach the Gospel. Jesus ridicules those who are concerned with titles, status, and honors. He castigates excessive concern for exoteric or "external" aspects of the tradition such as the strict enforcement of the rules of the purity system, and he indicts those who take pride in their own religiosity within the narrow boundaries of the world of comfort and conventional values. We may also note that these comments about the incompatibility of "wealth" and "serving God" need to be interpreted within the historical-cultural context of Jesus' time. Financial abundance, if based on honesty and integrity, can be most helpful when directed toward charitable causes and compassionate care for the greater good.

Jesus also questions the family as the primary social unit, and the only way for people to get a sense of identity and material security. He suggests that family ties can be a distraction and even an impediment to spiritual growth and progress. This info may come as a surprise, and even a shock. But Jesus refers to cases in which the family takes up one's *entire focus in life*. As a result, we may become totally oblivious to the suffering of others and ignore the greater common good. Jesus was not opposed to our loving our families — after all he spoke of loving everyone, even one's enemies — but his attitude toward family is not as uncritical and univocally affirmative as those who see Jesus as a champion of "family values" like to emphasize (see Luke 14:26 and Matt. 10:37). Indeed, according to Mark, Jesus' own family relations were strained.

In the Gospel of Mark, family is redefined as "those who do the will of God" (3:35), and the reference is to our "spiritual brothers and sisters" rather than to a "biological" family. The criticism of "earthly fathers and mothers" is emphasized in the Gnostic Gospel of Thomas where Jesus advocates a radical, countercultural life that aims right at the core of the patriarchal family unit that was ultimately a microcosmic reflection of the larger domination system of Jesus' ethnocentric society and culture. In fact, Jesus took a courageous stand against the absolute, dictatorial, coercive power of the human father, the head of the family, and it was an important part of his mission to replace this father-figure with the "heavenly Father," according to Huston Smith. Perhaps we can conclude that Jesus' position reflects an unconditional and boundless love that certainly includes the primary biological family, but also *transcends* it by extending beyond.

What is obvious is that Jesus challenged the central values of conventional wisdom prevalent in the society of his day: wealth, family, honor, purity, and religiosity.

In Luke, Jesus' ministry is more political than in the other Gospels; Luke's Jesus has an even stronger social agenda. He is portrayed as a "social prophet" in the tradition of the Jewish prophets Amos and Isaiah who challenged injustice, oppression, and any exploitation of the poor. In fact, it is remarkable how Luke's Jesus challenges the domination system of his day and reaches out to the stigmatized parts of society.

Interestingly, the social vision articulated in Luke is not exactly the same as that of the other synoptic Gospels. While we read "Blessed are you poor" and "Blessed are you who hunger and thirst" in Luke (6:20-26), in Matthew's famous version of the Sermon on the Mount these passages are altered: "Blessed are the poor *in spirit*, for theirs is the kingdom" (5:3) and "Blessed are those who hunger and thirst *for righteousness*" (5:6). One explanation has been that Matthew "spiritualizes" the blessings — also referred to as Beatitudes — so that they no longer refer to materially poor and hungry people. In *Things Hidden: Scripture as*

Spirituality, popular Franciscan teacher Richard Rohr argues that "poverty in spirit" refers to people who are overly complacent and self-righteous, hence lacking curiosity and open-heartedness. In other terms, those who have a "beginner's mind" similar to a child are the ones who are blessed. Other interpretations from scholars such as Marcus Borg suggest that Matthew refers to people whose material poverty has broken their spirit. Poverty — one of the great scourges of humanity — does not only undermine human dignity and the will to evolve spiritually, but it frequently also reduces life to a mere struggle for survival. This approach is reflected in Catholic social teachings. Since the end of the nineteenth century, a body of social doctrine has been developed by several popes on matters of poverty, wealth, economics, and social organization based on the principles of human dignity and solidarity. Borg reminds us that "righteousness" in the Bible does not mean personal rectitude, as it most often does in modern English, but justice. The meaning of Matthew's wording is thus similar — and maybe even identical — to the blessings in Luke, for it is the poor and needy who most yearn for justice.

Gender Complementarity

Jesus' closest following consisted of his inner circle, the twelve apostles who were mostly illiterate and came from the underprivileged rural population. Most of the apostles were day laborers; Simon Peter, for example, was a fisherman by trade. Whatever the case, church tradition stresses that Jesus had twelve *male* apostles. Yet, were the disciples of Jesus exclusively male? Modern research, including the evidence provided in the Gnostic scriptures, paints a different picture than the traditional view of the Church. Rosemary Radford Ruether, among other scholars, reminds us that the canonical Gospels record a significant circle of female disciples, with Mary Magdalene as their leader. Similarly, most of the Gnostic Gospels depict female disciples who travel with Jesus as equal members of his inner circle. All of the scriptures confirm that it is Mary Magdalene who is at Jesus' side during the crucifixion, and it is she who brings the good news of his resurrection to the male disciples who are all trembling in fear in the upper room. The Gospel narratives unanimously testify to the deep and pure soul love between Jesus and Mary Magdalene, attesting that it is on the basis of their profound mystical union that she is able to proclaim the resurrection. There is no doubt among scholars that Mary Magdalene was not only the chief of the disciples but a supreme adept in her own right and the receiver of some of Jesus' most intimate and advanced esoteric teachings. In fact, some sources describe Mary Magdalene as playing a leading role, that it was her job to correct misconceptions and bring higher vision to some of the male disciples. Why is this fact largely unknown in mainstream Christianity?

Orthodox Christianity as represented by the imperial Church marginalized these female disciples of Jesus by establishing the doctrine of "apostolic succession." The apostle Peter, the "rock" upon which the Church was to be founded (Matt. 16:18), was and still is considered to be the "first bishop of Rome" before he was martyred by crucifixion during the great persecution of Christians under the rule of Emperor Nero in the first century CE. Since the second century, the doctrine of "apostolic succession" has served to legitimize the authority of certain men who claimed to exercise exclusive leadership over the churches as the direct successors of Peter. This doctrine is the basis of papal authority to this day, as well as Eastern Orthodox claims to succession. It is also based on the more than questionable assumption that Jesus himself and *all* of his disciples were *exclusively male*.

Apostolic succession serves as the primary argument for the male priesthood. This doctrine continued the patriarchal order of cultural life in the first-century Mediterranean world. Though there were alternative voices within the Jewish tradition, the dominant paradigms of the time — which included Roman, Egyptian, Canaanite, Assyrian, Babylonian, Persian and Greek influences — largely disenfranchised women and favored men. Women had few, if any, of the rights men enjoyed. Women could not be witnesses in a court of law, nor could they initiate a divorce. They were not allowed to read the Torah, perhaps because the ability to read and interpret the Law was considered a source of empowerment. Women were physically separated from men in public life, and a woman's identity rested in either her father or her husband. Consequently, the privileges of shaping and articulating the Christian message over time were given to men with scribal power and leadership authority. Women's voices were minimized and marginalized.

It is not surprising, then, that many women were among Jesus' early and most devoted followers. Indeed, the role of women in the early Christian community is striking, and the stories of Jesus' interactions with women are most remarkable. For example, his interactions range from his defense of a woman accused of adultery to his socializing with prostitutes. Jesus himself violated Jewish convention by talking openly with women and by including them as his companions. His honoring of women outside of his circle of female disciples is perhaps most strikingly revealed in his interesting encounter with the Samaritan woman at the well who was considered an outcast because she had been married five times (she may have been either divorced or widowed). Her very presence at the well of Jacob potentially sullied the well. Yet Jesus chooses her to announce his true destiny. Moreover, when Jesus was hosted in the home of Mary and Martha, he affirmed Mary's role as a disciple. In fact, in all of his actions and teachings, and as a whole and unified being abiding in non-dual awareness, Jesus displayed a state of perfect psychospiritual integration of masculine and feminine archetypal energies.

In addition, the Gospels radicalize the "good news" by portraying outcast groups and people considered "ritually unclean" through several other female figures: The woman with the flow of blood, the widow, and the Syro-Phoenician woman. As members of despised groups, these women literally formed the bottom of the existing social hierarchy. Especially Luke's Jesus emphasizes the rights and needs of women. In a story found only in Luke, Mary is praised for not being concerned with her traditional "womanly" duties but for learning from her teacher, presumably along with the other disciples (10:38-42).

The early Christian vision was primarily based on the notion that "in Christ there is neither male nor female" — as Paul puts it in his *Letter to the Galatians* (3:28). Baptism into Christ was seen as making all humanity one in the image of God: male and female, Jew and Greek, slave and free. This revolutionary vision conferred a new status to all classes of society in Christ; in other words, Christ redeems all of humanity from its apparent divisions. The Jesus of the Gnostic Gospel of Thomas (sayings 22 and 114) makes it even clearer that it is not a matter of whether we are male or female, celibate or married, rich or poor. What matters is that we become a "living spirit." And a "living spirit" is a person who, like Jesus, has moved beyond the polar opposites and merged with his or her true Self. From a mystical-esoteric perspective, one can certainly argue that gender and class are ultimately irrelevant to spiritual evolution. This understanding of the basic equality of human souls and a shared humanity in the image of God was furthermore expressed in patterns of ministry that included women during the period of early Christianity. Women, together with men, were called to study and to teach the "new Torah" of Jesus. Some twenty years after Jesus' death, certain women even held positions of leadership in local Christian groups. Women acted as evangelists, prophetesses, deaconesses, and teachers. This clearly points to the radical social vision as embodied by the Christian movement in first-century Palestine, a movement that not only subverted the sharp social boundaries but also practiced a "discipleship of equals."

Communal Meals

Luke portrays "table fellowship" as a means of elucidating Jesus' way of teaching. Communal meals were central to Jesus' mission because of their symbolic significance. Sharing a meal created new bonds of friendship, hence reaffirming God's love and presence even in the most mundane and simple activities. When meals included people beyond the biological family, they lifted social boundaries. In other words, to share a meal was a form of social inclusion. Jesus repeatedly shares meals with outcasts such as tax collectors and others previously considered "sinners" and "impure." The communal meals of Jesus embodied his vision of a more loving and inclusive society. As Marcus Borg puts it: "The ethos of compassion led to an inclusive table fellowship, just as the ethos of purity led to a closed table fellowship."[14] Not surprisingly, Jesus' table fellowship with marginalized groups drew strong criticism and became a source of permanent conflict.

The "Kingdom of God" — in Heaven or on Earth?

(Author's note: I've included a brief discussion of Apocalyptic thought here in *Jesus Christ: The Love and Wisdom of a First-Century Mystic*. For a compelling and in-depth focus on the Christian Book of Revelation and other Apocalyptic Prophesies, please refer to my e-book, *Visions of the End: The Christian Book of Revelation and other Apocalyptic Prophesies*, which can be found in the *One Truth, Many Paths: Isabella Price's Cross-Cultural Guides to Human Spirituality Series*.)

By the time of Jesus, there had been revelations and visions portending a time in which wrongdoers would be judged. Jewish thought at this time was influenced by Zoroastrianism, an ancient Persian religion, as some Jews lived under Persian rule during the post-exilic period beginning in 538 BCE. In Zoroastrianism and the monotheistic belief systems it influenced, two supreme forces of reality are contending with each other for control of the universe: the forces of good and evil. It was thought that this conflict would lead to a complete reversal of the present order. An apocalyptical judgment day was widely believed to be imminent during the lifetime of Jesus, as is reflected especially in the Gospel of Mark. As a preacher of repentance like his predecessor John the Baptist, Mark's Jesus taught that the Kingdom of God was at hand. The first words in Mark can be read as a testimony of this worldview: "The time has been fulfilled, the Kingdom of God is near; repent and believe in the good news" (Mark 1:15). We are told in Mark that Jesus addressed his followers by telling them that they would not taste death until they saw the Kingdom of God come in power (Mark 13:1-37).

Similarly, today's apocalyptic Christians believe that the end of the age, the Final Judgment and the Second Coming are imminent, including the belief that Jesus will return physically to raise the dead from their graves. However, their way of telling Jesus' story does not emphasize the world-centric compassionate Jesus who was a friend of *all* humanity, including "sinners" and outcasts, but rather the ethno-centric "warrior" Christ of the Book of Revelation. This apocalyptic worldview, which reflects primarily the mythic-traditional stage of consciousness and culture, tends to draw a strict line between believers and unbelievers, righteous and wicked, and so forth. Moreover, this worldview harbors the potential for a relative disregard of the state of affairs of *this* world. Justice, peace, and the preservation of nature lose their significance if everything is going to end soon anyway.

Unlike Mark's Gospel, we find no emphasis on the apocalyptic notion that the end of the world is imminent in Luke. For Luke, the end could not have been imminent when Jesus was teaching, since he knew by the time he wrote his Gospel that it had not (yet) occurred. In addition, Jesus' message had to first be taken into the world with the explicit purpose of bringing salvation to both Jews *and* Gentiles in fulfillment of God's plan. This explains why Luke has a stronger social agenda than the other Gospels. For Luke, the Kingdom of God was already at hand in Jesus. The Gospel of Luke simply says that "those who suffer now will be blessed then" (Luke 6:20-23).

What are the different layers of interpretation that can be applied to those passages that reassure the followers of Jesus that the "Kingdom of God" is imminent? While the Kingdom of God, as described in the canonical Gospels, has been mostly understood as a *future* cataclysmic event, a state yet to come consistent with apocalyptic logic, this is by no means the only possible interpretation. Let us consider alternatives. What if the "Kingdom of God" is not an eschatological Kingdom but is, in fact, *already existing on earth* and humans just don't see or realize it? The Gnostic Gospels of Thomas and Mary offer some interesting insights in this connection, and can be compared to Luke. According to Thomas, Jesus said:

> "If your leaders say to you, 'Look the kingdom is in heaven', then the birds of heaven will precede you. If they say to you, 'It is in the sea', then the fish will precede you. But the kingdom is in you and outside you. When you know yourselves, you will be known,

and you will understand that you are children of the living Father." (3)

When the disciples asked Jesus when the Kingdom of God would come, Jesus replied:

> "It will not come because you are looking for it. No one will announce, 'Look, here it is', or 'Look, there it is.' Rather, the Father's kingdom is spread out over the earth, and people do not see it." (113)

The Gospel of Mary affirms this understanding: "Be on your guard so that no one deceives you by saying, 'Look over here' or 'Look over there.' For the Child of Humanity exists *within* you. Follow it. Those who search for it will find it" (8:15-17). Similarly, Luke states: "The kingdom of God is not coming in an observable way. Nor will people say, 'Look, here it is," or 'There it is!' For look, the kingdom of God is inside you." (17:20-21).

According to these passages in Thomas, Mary, and Luke, the Kingdom of God is not to be understood in literal terms, as a specific geographical location "up in the sky" or "in heaven," nor is it necessarily a future event. Rather, the Kingdom is *within* us as well as *without*. It is neither "here" nor "there" but everywhere. God is not "hidden in heaven" and not separate from creation. In the Gospel of Thomas, Jesus also says: "Split a piece of wood, and I am there. Lift up the stone, and you will find me there" (77). God is transcendent *and* immanent in everything and every being. In the Gospels of Thomas and Mary, Jesus is not the exalted apocalyptic son of man coming at the end of time to usher in a new era because God's Kingdom *exists already in the here and now*. Thomas and Mary describe the Kingdom primarily as a process of self-discovery that involves a transformed consciousness. God can also be found *within* our own selves. Indeed, this reflects the "original blessing" that Self-knowledge is knowledge of God, as discussed. Thus, the Kingdom of which Jesus spoke may very well be a "Kingdom of Wisdom" rather than a Kingdom coming with the fires of Judgment Day. This new stage of the evolution of consciousness and culture has the potential to heal society as a whole from its rifts and divisions. The Kingdom of Wisdom is a society inaugurated by Jesus in *this* world. It is a society in which clean and unclean, poor and rich, male and female, righteous and sinners are all equally embraced by God's unconditional love. Divine love is the matrix, the ground of being that always was, is, and will be. And all of nature's exquisite beauty surrounding us is equally included: the birds of the air and the lilies of the field. The Kingdom of God is a real "Kingdom" right here on earth. It is a Kingdom where the first will be last and the last first. The establishment of God's Kingdom and the vindication of the righteous is *already happening*. What "will be" already *is* — for those who have eyes to see, ears to hear, and hearts to understand. The Kingdom is a society in which humans have consciously realized the profound meaning of interrelatedness on a collective scale by transcending all forms of separation. To take this vision a step further, it is a society in which humans have become fully aware of their potential for actively and creatively participating in the evolutionary process as responsible and engaged co-creators. What integral theory and spiral dynamics refer to as "Second Tier" beginning with the *integral* stage of consciousness and culture, is, from a Christian perspective, the Kingdom of Wisdom initiated by the "Kosmic Christ" who *is* the sacred evolutionary impulse that drives the perpetual unfolding of all that is.

Reaching the "Kingdom of God"

To reach the "Kingdom of God" is the goal of a Christian life. Millions of Christians still believe that this means primarily "going to Heaven" and reaping the rewards *after death*. Yet others envision the Kingdom as a utopian community based on love, tolerance, and mutual respect. However, when looking at all of the Gospels, canonical and non-canonical, the concept remains ambiguous and multi-faceted. In fact, figuring out exactly what Jesus meant still divides contemporary scholarship. Some scholars argue that Jesus was convinced that the Kingdom would come in the near future by means of a dramatic intervention by God, a position referred to as "apocalyptic eschatology" (or, end-time theology). Other scholars make the case that Jesus' language about the Kingdom is to be understood within a framework that involves human collaboration with God. However, this can only happen if humans are sufficiently empowered to become conscious co-creators and participants in the unfolding of the sacred evolutionary impulse. For conscious and fully awakened participation in evolution, humans need to embody a Second Tier integrated stage of consciousness and culture.

Overall, we can conclude that at least as much evidence in

the Gospels points to the "Kingdom of God" as a metaphor for more evolved stages of consciousness as it does to a literal traditional-conventional interpretation. Interestingly, the primary disagreement among scholars is not about the *content* of what the "Kingdom of God" would look like, but about *how* and *when* Jesus thought it would become reality. Did Jesus expect God to intervene, and if so, soon? Or did he expect humans to actively collaborate with God to make the new Kingdom a reality? Widespread agreement exists among progressive scholars on both sides of the division that God's Kingdom was meant *for the earth* and was not about "heaven." In addition, scholars mostly agree that the "Kingdom of God" was a term with political and religious implications — two domains of life that were interrelated in Jewish culture and society. Similarly, Roman imperial theology combined religion and politics in the notion of the emperor's divinity, a notion that served to legitimize the political and socio-cultural order imposed by Rome. Consequently, Jesus' use of kingdom language carried a political edge that clearly challenged the domination systems of his world. Marcus Borg argues that as a political-religious metaphor the Kingdom of God referred to what life would be like on earth if God was king and the worldly kingdoms did not exist. To a certain extent, Jesus' use of the term "Kingdom of God" thus subverted and even negated the kingdoms of his day by affirming a different king and kingdom.

During the Middle Ages, underprivileged groups of the population — most prominently the peasants — were taught by the imperial Church to accept the existing social order and to endure their dire life circumstances for the sake of salvation in the afterlife. Thus, individualized salvation became one of the main preoccupations in Western Christianity. The "privatization of religion" generally served the political and economic agenda of the Church, which was in a convenient alliance with ruling elites. The ruling establishment had a vested interest in preventing people from seeing themselves as conscious agents of justice and social transformation. This preoccupation with individualized salvation, based on the alluring promise of generous compensation in an alleged afterlife, was indeed a far cry from the revolutionary teachings of Jesus Christ that had placed significant emphasis on social reforms and justice in *this world*.

Matthew Fox reminds us that Jesus Christ does indeed call all persons to be compassionate transformers of society by alleviating the pain of those who suffer. Jesus' social gospel was perhaps most prominently put into practice by the medieval monasteries, a dominant fixture in the social and cultural life of Europe. While the leaders of the medieval Church hierarchy constituted an integral part of the ruling elite, the monasteries as such provided valuable social services. They served, for example, as orphanages and places of refuge for individuals suffering from natural or other calamities. They often provided food for the poor and medical treatment for the ill and injured.

Today, most biblical scholars agree that the "Kingdom of God" was not only for this world but also involved such a *transformed* world, a utopian vision brought about by God. This vision implies the end of violence, war, and injustice, the liberation from bondage, and the healing from paralysis and blindness.

This transformed world is also a world of plenty where milk and honey flow abundantly, everybody will have enough, and the poor and outcasts will be served and cared for first. This is a world of selfless service where those who want to be the greatest are told, "if anyone wants to be first, he must make himself last of all and *servant* of all" (Mark 9:35). Finally, it is a society of fully awakened humans beyond the constraints of the time-space-continuum. The "Kingdom" is to be found neither in the past nor in the future but in the eternal here and now.

Just as Jesus spoke of imitating God's compassion, he also spoke of participating in God's justice in the context of community. In the Acts of the Apostles we read, for example, that the early Christians were united in their hearts and that this bond found its expression in strong mutual support. We learn that "not one of these early Christians claimed any of his possessions as his own" (Acts 4:32). In fact, those who owned property would frequently share their goods with all the needy members of the community to provide for their basic necessities. The distribution of goods to any members in need, however, does not necessarily imply that early Christians rendered themselves destitute. The text of Acts seems to imply that they let go of what they didn't really need. When reading these passages and examining how modern and post-modern Western society operates, one can't help but wonder how far from these ideals the so-called "Christian world" has veered. Partly, this is the result of capitalism and the industrial revolution that initiated the modernist stage of consciousness and culture in the West. Moreover, the Calvinist belief in predestination, that is, the belief that economic prosperity and material success proved that one was chosen by God for special blessings, likely stimulated the growth of capitalism. Yet, Jesus' teachings reveal a different picture. In another passage in the Gospels, in which Jesus speaks of human worries about food and clothing, he admonishes his followers: "Set your mind on God's kingdom and his justice before everything else, and all the rest will come to you as well" (Matt. 6:33; Luke 12:31). This passage aims right at the core of Jesus' passion for the Kingdom of God that implied a transformed world.

The Sacrifice of the Only Son of God

The story of the passion, death and resurrection of Jesus Christ is certainly one of the best-known stories on earth. It constitutes the central drama of the Gospels. While the basic plot of the story is the same in all of the Gospels, the details vary. For example, Luke's passion account follows the same storyline as in Matthew and Mark, but presents Jesus as a figure who is in control of his feelings, exercises authority to the end without any signs of agony, and dies with a prayer of acceptance on his lips. However, the Gospel of Mark — which has sometimes been called a "passion narrative with a long introduction" — portrays Jesus in a different light. In Mark, nobody seems to understand who Jesus is. After much rejection, pain, and suffering, Jesus cries out in despair at the cross: "My God, my God, why have you forsaken me?"(15:34) But while Matthew and Luke follow Mark's narrative with minor modifications, John's version of the story — as we have seen — is quite different.

As we noted earlier, in the final week of his life, Jesus and his followers come to Jerusalem to celebrate Passover. He enters the holy city in a manner designed to evoke the prophecy of Zechariah (9:9): "See, your king is coming to you ... humble and mounted on a donkey." The sight of Jesus, now a well-known healer and teacher, attracts large crowds of people interested in hearing his message and perhaps witnessing a great miracle. The crowds spread their garments before him and hail him with hosannas. The Temple authorities get nervous and they fear a riot. Several acts performed by Jesus — such as, for example, the cleansing of the Temple, and the urging to devalue Roman leadership in favor of a Kingdom of God — are perceived as a threat to the status quo. They know that many in the crowd are eager for a change in their dire life circumstances. The authorities thus seek a way to arrest Jesus. On Wednesday, Judas, one of Jesus' disciples, provides the opportunity. He meets with the authorities and agrees to betray Jesus (Mark 14:10-11). Much has been speculated about this based on the meager details provided in the story, yet we do not really know the motive for Judas's betrayal.

On Thursday, Jesus has a final meal with his followers. In the synoptic Gospels, this meal is a Passover Seder celebrating ancient Israel's liberation from Egypt. In John's Gospel, however, the occasion is not the feast of Passover; the Passover meal actually takes place the next evening, and thus the lambs to be eaten at the meal are killed at the hour of Jesus' death, which occurs late in the afternoon. That may explain John's references to Jesus Christ as the sacrificial "Lamb of God" (1:29 and 1:36).

Jesus as "God's Lamb" is foreshadowed by the substitution of a ram (an adult male lamb) for Isaac's sacrifice in Genesis; Jewish tradition links the lamb of the original Passover to Abraham's son Isaac as the "perfect sacrifice" on Mt. Moriah (Gen.22). The thematic connections between Abraham's willingness to offer his "only son" (by Sarah) and God's willingness to offer his "only son" are obvious: "God so loved the world that he gave his *only Son*" (John 3:16). Moreover, Isaac's willingness to be the sacrifice prefigures Jesus' voluntary act of self-sacrifice in Christian understanding.

At the "Last or Lord's Supper," Jesus moves beyond the traditional understanding of Passover. He sees to it that wine and bread are provided, and as he shares this with his disciples, he explains with great solemnity that the bread and wine represent *his* body and blood. In Matthew, Jesus even refers to the cup of wine as the "blood of the covenant" (26:28). This is consistent with Matthew's portrayal of Jesus as the "new Moses," echoing the confirmation of the covenant at the time of Moses as described in Exodus (24:8). Another difference is that in the Christian tradition Jesus' blood is perceived as being more valuable than the blood of sacrificial animals in previous religious rites, because this sacrifice needed to be performed only *once*.

The "sacrifice of God's only Son" is a theme particularly emphasized in John. Later, it became the foundation of the post-Easter Christology. While the synoptic Gospels affirm that Jesus was the "Son of God," it is important to emphasize that they do *not* present this affirmation as part of Jesus' own message — unlike John. In Mark, for example, it is the Roman centurion, the commander of the soldiers who crucified Jesus, who exclaims:

"This man must have been a son of God" (15:39). Interestingly enough, this statement by a Roman commander strongly challenges imperial ideology stressing the divinity of the emperor. Yet Jesus' followers do not make the same claim in Mark. We have no way of knowing as we read Mark whether Jesus thought of himself as the "Son of God." According to the earliest layers of the emerging Gospel tradition that are represented in this Gospel, the pre-Easter Jesus made no specific references or comments that would confirm such a claim. Jesus did not claim special status, and instead pointed away from himself to God.

Of course, great differences exist between the Abrahamic traditions as to *how* the term "Son of God" is to be understood as applied to Jesus. Karen Armstrong reminds us that "the Christian doctrine of the Incarnation of God in Jesus has always scandalized Jews, and, later, Muslims would also find it blasphemous."[15] Muslims acknowledge Jesus' great significance, but only as a mortal, miracle-working prophet. Muslims believe that both Jesus and Mohammed were very great prophets, but that God did not have a son. Christians believe that Jesus is the only Son of God, the Messiah, the Anointed One, and absolutely and unquestionably divine. Jews believe that every human (including non-Jews) is a child of God. The Jewish Talmud, written shortly after the birth of Jesus, and which may reflect the Jewish teaching of Jesus' time, says that human parents give a child her or his physical form, but that God — who does not have a gender or physical representation — gives every child his or her intelligence, personality, and soul.

The Church Council of Nicaea (325 CE) declared Jesus to be

both *fully human* and *fully divine*. According to Christian belief, only *one* God exists; yet, in that one God are *three* distinct divine Persons — the Father, the Son, and the Holy Spirit — each of whom possess equally and eternally the same divine substance (i.e., *ousia* in Greek) and energy (i.e., *energeia* in Greek). In other words, the Christian God is "three-in-one, yet undivided." This is in sharp contrast to the Islamic view of God as one and wholly indivisible; and Judaism's conception of God as one, whole and infinite entity.

The theological conviction that Jesus Christ is the preexistent "Son of God the Father," that is, the literal Second Person of the Trinity who combines two natures (human *and* divine) within his being, was essential in shaping Christian doctrine down through the centuries. Not only did the Nicene Creed — together with the Church Council of Chalcedon in 451 CE that hammered out the doctrine of the Holy Trinity — define orthodoxy for all time... but its recitation in Christian services over the centuries deeply ingrained a "Son of God" Christology within the collective psyche of Western culture. However, it needs to be reemphasized that this had *not yet* happened during the first decades of Christianity. When the New Testament was written, no official Christology existed, and perceptions of Jesus had not yet crystallized into doctrines. A number of documents in the New Testament suggest that rudimentary forms of creedal statements may have existed in the first century (commonly referred to as the Apostles' Creed). For example, Paul's *Letter to the Philippians* (2:5-8) describes how Jesus "emptied himself" of all divine prerogatives, and how he humbled himself and shared the human lot even to the point of dying on the cross. In this context, Huston Smith reminds us that it was Jesus' humanity (and not his divinity) that had to be argued for in the Greco-Roman world. The Gospel of Matthew, composed likely between 70 and 90 CE, shows Jesus sending his followers to baptize "all nations in the name of the Father, the Son, and the Holy Spirit" (28:19) — an early reference to the later notion of the Trinity.

In early Christianity, alternative images of Jesus existed as well. Along with the son/father imagery found in the New Testament that later served as foundation for the Son of God-Christology of the emerging imperial Church, we find, for example, the image of Jesus as an embodiment of divine wisdom, as we have already established. In the light of this evidence from the early Christian period, Marcus Borg suggests that Jesus may not be thought of exclusively as the Son of God in a *literal* sense but rather as one whose relationship to God was so intimate and profound that he could be spoken of, *metaphorically*, as the "Son of God" and "the Child of Wisdom or Sophia." Borg's suggestion is consistent with the Jewish culture within which Jesus was born, however this idea is inconsistent with what Christians believe is essential, namely, that Jesus was *literally* the "Son of God." In addition, Borg argues that a literal reading of Jesus as the "Son of God" narrows the scope and richness of early Christological images and expressions by focusing on just *one* particular image. Moreover, this focus on one image leads to endless arguments over the question of whether one *believes* that Jesus was literally and exclusively the "Son of God." Finally, uncertainty as to what, exactly, is being affirmed when one argues that Jesus literally is the "Son of God" needs to be taken into consideration as well.

Yet with all of that said, we should not forget that all theological constructs — no matter how elaborate and sophisticated they may be — ultimately never adequately express the nature of the ineffable divine mystery. In this context, it is interesting to note that contemporary Christian scholars and teachers, drawing from the contemplative Christian tradition, have suggested alternative interpretations of the Trinity. In *The Wisdom Jesus*, Cynthia Bourgeault reminds us that the Trinity is really an "icon of self-emptying love" when understood in a wisdom sense. The Trinity may then be seen as a continuous outpouring of divine love from the Father to the Son, from the Son to the Spirit, and from the Spirit back to the Father. As the "three persons" constantly overspill into one another, the energy of love becomes manifest and accessible. Franciscan teacher Richard Rohr also emphasizes this interpretation of the Trinity, hence connecting Christianity to its deepest wisdom roots *and* to the fluid, relational nature of consciousness itself as reflected in Eastern spiritual traditions and modern quantum physics. Viewed from this perspective, God's love is in constant motion and becomes manifest as the unified field of all reality.

Crosses on a hill, no copyright assignation,
procured online through Creative Commons

Arrest and Crucifixion

After the Last Supper, Jesus and his disciples leave the city and go to the Garden of Gethsemane at the foot of the Mount of Olives just east of the walls of Jerusalem. Here the reports of the synoptic Gospels differ. Mark has Jesus agonizing over his impending death, while Luke's Jesus displays calmness and sovereignty. Mark's Jesus appears to delve deeply into the dark night of the soul. His feelings of being utterly abandoned by God are furthermore compounded by Judas's arrival in the dark with a group of armed men as Jesus' other disciples flee. The Gospels report that Jesus is arrested and taken to a hearing before the Temple authorities, presided over by Caiaphas, the high priest. He asks Jesus if he is the prophesied Messiah. Jesus' answer is somewhat ambiguous. The hearing ends with Jesus being accused of blasphemy, an accusation that incurs the death sentence. However, great historical uncertainty exists about this scene before the high council. One of the main reasons is that it would have taken place at night and on the day of the most important Jewish festival of the year when trials were forbidden. Another reason is that Jesus' response to the questions of the high priest amounts to an early Christian confession of faith remarkably reminiscent of post-Easter proclamations about Jesus.

At dawn on Friday, the Temple authorities turn Jesus over to Pilate, the Roman governor of Judea. The synoptic Gospels all report that Pilate asks Jesus: "Are you the King of the Jews?" Jesus replies: "The words are yours." Then Jesus remains silent and refuses to respond to any further questions.

Being "King of the Jews" was a claim the authorities had to take seriously. From a Roman perspective, this leadership position challenged the emperor as the "only king" and amounted to an act of political insurgency. The Kingdom Jesus spoke about, however, was not to be implemented by an act of political rebellion. It appears unlikely that Jesus publicly declared himself "king" during his ministry, nor is there evidence that Jesus called himself the Messiah in public, although his followers likely thought of him in this way. In fact, the three synoptic Gospels affirm that Jesus is the Messiah, yet they do not present this as part of his own message. Mark, for example, reports Peter's affirmation "You are the Messiah" (8:29). In ancient Israel the term "Messiah," which means the "anointed one" (the Greek term for Messiah is *Christos*), was one of the designations of the "future king." But while Jesus may have spoken of himself as the Messiah in private with his disciples, he did not declare that he would drive out the Romans and restore Israel to sovereignty. Rather, he suggested in his comments that God was eventually going to overthrow the forces of evil. After Jesus' death, his disciples continued to call him the Messiah — even though in general Jews at that time did not believe that the Messiah was supposed to suffer and die. The Talmud predicts that the Messiah will usher in an era of freedom, peace, and goodness for all humankind. By the time of Jesus, Messianic hope had become greatly politicized in the minds of the people. Resistance against Roman rule had crystallized around the expectation of a Messianic figure who would eliminate the oppressive powers altogether and restore Israel among the nations. One small and no-longer existent sect of Judaism, that existed shortly after the death of Jesus, the Zealots, believed that Israel should be taken back by force from the Roman rulers. Their rebellion against Rome failed and led to the destruction of the Second Temple in Jerusalem by Roman forces during the Jewish War (66-70 CE). This hope for a "political" rather than a "spiritual" Messiah later culminated in the acceptance of the "political Messiah" Bar Kochba — who led another revolt against Rome in the years 132-135 CE.

It is interesting to note that members of a group called "Jews for Jesus" continue to make the case that Jesus was, in fact, the prophesied Messiah. They base their arguments primarily on criteria and characteristics of the Messiah found in the Jewish scriptures and argue that as to lineage, birthplace, time in history, and lifestyle, Jesus matches the Messianic expectations of the scriptures in detail. This viewpoint is rejected by mainstream Judaism.

The interrogation with Pilate is followed by a curious episode involving Barabbas, a Jewish insurrectionist awaiting execution. Pilate offers the crowd that is present in the courtyard of Pilate's residence a choice between Jesus and Barabbas. The crowd chooses Barabbas and demands Jesus' crucifixion. However, the crowd that has entered the courtyard is a small one. It appears to be quite a different crowd from the one that had listened to Jesus just a few days earlier and whom the authorities feared. Pilate issues the order to have Jesus crucified together with two criminals. Crucifixion at that time was a commonly practiced form of imperial execution. Rome reserved crucifixion primarily for chronically defiant slaves and all others who challenged the Roman domination system. In this context, it is interesting to note that there are some differences between the synoptic Gospels when it comes to the events leading up to Pilate's death sentence. In contrast to Matthew, who puts the blame on the *entire population*, Luke reports that it is the *ruling establishment* that works against Jesus and plots his death. After Pilate issues the death sentence, Jesus is flogged, hit, and spit upon. Soldiers mock him as a would-be "King of the Jews," dress him in a purple cloak and adorn his head with a crown of thorns. John reports that Jesus carries the cross himself and is taken to a place called the "Skull," or "Golgotha" in Hebrew, where he is crucified.

    Yet again, the Gospels differ in their accounts of Jesus' last hours on the cross. Mark, for example, reports the crucifixion in one single sentence stating that "it was nine in the morning when they crucified him" (15:25) and does not narrate the details of what this kind of death entailed. At noon, darkness falls over the entire land and lasts until Jesus' death three hours later. At three,

Jesus cries out in his final agony reported by both Mark and Matthew: "My God, my God, why have you forsaken me?" (Mark 15:34; Matt.27:46) After that, he dies. In Luke, however, Jesus' last words are: "Father, into your hands I commit my spirit" (23:46). The three hours of darkness are reported in all the synoptic Gospels. Different scientific theories have been used to explain the darkness as a historical-factual event. However, the idea of darkness can equally be understood as a metaphor. In ancient times, darkness was an archetypal symbol related to grief, suffering, and God's judgment. For example, evidence can be found in Exodus where one of the ten plagues brought darkness over the entire land of Egypt. In the Torah, judgment upon Israel is frequently announced by the prophets with the impending threat of God "darkening the earth in broad daylight" (Amos 8:9). The darkness clearly implies cosmic dimensions; the universe itself joins in mourning the passion and death of the savior. Jesus now came to be understood by his followers as the "new suffering servant," a reference to the exilic prophet second Isaiah (42:1) who spoke of the people of Israel as a suffering "servant" during the period of the Babylonian Exile a few hundred years earlier.

Risen from the Dead

The story of Jesus' death and resurrection dominates Christian thought and constitutes the core message of Easter. The common understanding of Easter combines the stories found in all the Gospels into a composite whole and perceives them through the lens of Christian teachings. Three basic claims stand out: First,

Jesus' tomb was found empty; second, this was the case because God had raised Jesus from the dead; and third, Jesus appeared to his followers after his death in a form that could be seen, heard, and touched — as attested by several witnesses. In fact, "for many Christians the historical factuality of the Easter stories is so central that if it didn't happen this way, the foundation and truth of Christianity would disappear."[16] But by focusing exclusively on the factuality of these Easter stories, we risk missing their deeper metaphorical meaning, and reduce them to a mere matter of debate as to whether we *believe* or *not* that the tomb was really empty, or whether the testimony of eyewitnesses can truly stand up to the criteria of historical inquiry, as Marcus Borg argues. To understand the Easter stories as metaphorical narratives, however, does *not* imply a denial of their factuality. It just puts a greater emphasis on the *meaning* while leaving the question of historical factuality open. Moreover, we need to be aware of the fact that, right from the start, accounts and interpretations varied of what it meant to say that Jesus had risen from the dead. Let us now examine some fundamental aspects as to how resurrection was understood in the Judeo-Christian traditions.

The culture in which Jesus lived did not place much emphasis on the question of a possible afterlife. Jesus' resurrection was proclaimed from the start primarily from two perspectives: First, a just God had vindicated the death of a righteous, innocent man and restored justice that had been upset by the tragedy of his crucifixion. Second, the followers of Jesus continued to experience his presence after his death. Indeed, they experienced him as a divine reality, as one with God. The resurrection provided evidence that Jesus was a figure with a broader role in world history. The risen Christ could become the "living Christ."

As we have pointed out, different layers of interpretation evolved over time, as is apparent in the Gospels. In Mark, the focus is largely on the vindication of the righteous "Son of Man." Jesus predicts his own death three times, stating that the Son of Man must suffer death and be raised in three days. Mark mentions the women — Mary Magdalene, Mary the mother of James, and Salome — who witness Jesus' death and seek out the tomb to anoint his body. When they arrive, they realize that the large stone at the entrance has been removed and that the tomb is empty. A young man, sitting next to the tomb and dressed in a white robe, says, "Jesus of Nazareth, who was crucified, has been raised" (Mark 16:6). Mark's narrative is brief. The other Gospels add more narrative details to the story. Matthew, for example, explains that guards had been posted at the entrance of the tomb and that an angel had removed the stone from the entrance. Matthew, Luke, and John also differ from Mark in that they report multiple appearances of the risen Jesus; in Mark, however, no appearances are mentioned. Matthew includes a story that fulfills Jesus' promise of making an appearance on a mountaintop in Galilee. It is there that the risen Jesus proclaims the words that came to be known as the "Great Commission" — Jesus has been given "all authority in heaven and on earth," and his followers are "to make disciples of all nations" (28:18-19). Matthew concludes with a promise of the risen Christ: "I am with you always" (28:20). The risen Christ *is* God's abiding presence; he is "God with us." Luke tells another story of the risen Jesus who encounters two of his followers as they walk from Jerusalem to a village named Emmaus. The two men are suddenly joined by a stranger whom the reader knows to be the risen Christ. Jesus' followers, however, don't recognize him at first. Only when the stranger takes the bread, blesses it, and breaks it, do they finally realize that it is Jesus Christ. Whether the encounter occurred or not in a literal-factual sense, will always remain a matter of debate. The profound message of this story as a metaphorical narrative is, however, that the encounter on the road to Emmaus happens again and again because Jesus *is* the Christ consciousness within us. He calls us into profound and authentic relationships. He lives, suffers, and dies with us on the many roads and turns our lives eventually take — even if we do not recognize him. Our task is simply to open our eyes, to see with our hearts.

Finally, to mention one more example, John reports the story of "doubting Thomas." Jesus appears to the disciples in a house with locked doors on the evening of Easter Sunday (20:19-29). The story of Thomas is a great testament to the post-Easter Christian confession of faith: Jesus is Lord, he is risen, and he lives. He is *not* a figure of the past but of the eternal, timeless present.

What is the truth about the resurrection? Did it really happen, and how could the risen Christ possibly exist as a "body?" From a historical perspective, it is impossible to say what really happened and, perhaps, not even helpful to ask. Too much has already been written and speculated about possible Passover plots. Short of divine revelation or personal faith, we simply don't know and can't know exactly what happened after Jesus was entombed. In the end, the resurrection likely remains a matter of belief that lies beyond the scope of historical inquiry, as Bart Ehrman concludes. Other scholars such as Huston Smith put the situation as follows: "Jesus appears to have been resurrected (but) his resurrected body differed importantly from the one that died on the cross. It was visible: some people recognized it as that of the Jesus they knew. And it was corporeal: the resurrected Jesus hungered and ate, and Thomas touched the spear wound in his side. At the same time, it was incorporeal: it passed through closed doors. These mysterious differences persuaded the disciples that their Master had entered a new mode of being."[17] For Paul, who felt that he himself had an experience of the risen Jesus after a vision on the road to Damascus, resurrection involved not a body of flesh, but an imperishable, spiritual body (1 Cor.15: 42-51). Consequently, when Paul described the Church as the "body of Christ," he introduced an interpretation which was much more consistent with Hellenistic schools of thought that drew a sharp distinction between the perishable flesh and the imperishable soul of a person. In this context, resurrection meant that the imperishable soul received an imperishable body — not one of corruptible flesh. This imperishable "body of Christ" was to be found in his people and in his teachings, among others. The first Christians — Paul being the most prominent among them — who spread the Christian message through the Mediterranean world to the Gentiles, strongly felt that Jesus was in their midst as a concrete energizing power. They remembered that he had said where two or three were gathered in his name, he would be there among them. The human form of Jesus Christ had left the earth, yet he continued his uncompleted mission through a new and imperishable body, that is, the Church of which he remained the head.

In the end, the answer to the question as to whether the risen Jesus exists as a "body" remains, naturally, elusive. The Gospel writers primarily interpreted the Hebraic idea of bodily resurrection within the context of Hellenistic culture, that is, they avoided making the risen Christ a totally disembodied spirit. However, if the risen Jesus existed as a body, it was certainly a body so radically *different* from any meaning we usually attribute to the word "body" that it seems misleading to even use the term. As already established, Paul himself comes closest to this understanding when he speaks of it as a "spiritual body" and explicitly contrasts it to the "physical body of flesh and blood" (1 Cor. 15:44-50).

Clearly, the concept of the risen Jesus transcends our categories and our understanding of a physical body and implies that the body is not confined by time and space. In this context, we may also refer to Jesus' resurrected body as a more subtle body, or a "body of light" very different from the physical body. The Gnostics who lived at the time of Jesus commonly rejected and even ridiculed the idea of bodily resurrection because they considered the material world to be deeply flawed and corruptible. However, they had a complex and nuanced conception of spiritual reincarnation. Finally, we may add that it is not necessary to take the resurrection literally to take it seriously. With the evolution of consciousness and culture throughout time and history, changing attitudes toward the body, sexuality, death, and love have influenced new understandings of the claim to Jesus' resurrection. To whatever extent resurrection may remain controversial, the truth is that those who witnessed the resurrection were all deeply transformed by this experience. Indeed, resurrection is a concept of sublime hope and optimism that locates redemption where ultimate horror also resides, that is, in pain, mutilation, and death.

Jesus' Death — Substitutionary Atonement for our Sins?

The popular understanding of Christianity to the present day has been dominated by the image of Jesus as the dying and resurrecting savior and by the cross as the central symbol of his suffering. Jesus' obedience unto death exemplified the proper spiritual attitude that served as a guideline for all Christian communities. His death was regarded as the ultimate sacrifice for the love of God. Thus, the religious zeal of early Christians became infused with the notion that the willingness to suffer demonstrated moral strength. This attitude became especially apparent during the great persecutions of Christians by some of the more notorious Roman emperors in the decades after Jesus' death. Rather than giving up their faith, many of these early Christians willingly chose martyrdom and death.

Introducing the Idea of Original Sin

Many Christians believe that death itself and all human suffering arose only after Adam chose to sin. While the first Adam committed a transgression that led to humanity's fall, Jesus Christ — sometimes referred to as the "second Adam" — atoned for that sin with his death and thus redeemed humanity. For most Christians, the fall is inseparable from the redemption provided by Christ, that is, the act by which human souls are washed clean of the stain of original sin. Original sin — an integral part of the doctrine of the Fall — implies that Adam and Eve fell from perfection and brought evil into a perfect world because they had disobeyed God. However it was not until hundreds of years *after* Jesus' death that original sin was officially adopted as a Church doctrine. Though the origins of this doctrine are controversial, it was St. Augustine (354-430 CE), bishop of Hippo (modern-day Algeria), who largely devised it by drawing from the Pauline letters. For example, one of the passages in Paul's *Letter to the Romans* states: "For through the disobedience of one man many were made sinners, so through the obedience of one man many will be made righteous" (5:19). Another passage from Romans addresses the perennial question of the human free will — a question that also relates to the doctrine of original sin: "I do not even acknowledge my own actions as mine, for what I do is not what I want to do, but what I detest." (7:15) It is from these passages, and from other sources — including his own life experience — that Augustine came to believe that our human experiences and actions are not only *apart* from but even *against* our will. For Augustine, the human will as an instrument of free choice and agent of transformation becomes thus obsolete. Augustine argued that Adam and Eve had originally been given free will but that they later changed the structure of the universe through an act based on the same free will. It was their willful choice — the so-called "original sin" — that had brought mortality and sexual desire upon the human race, and, in the process, had deprived Adam's progeny of the freedom to choose not to sin. In other terms, because Adam's original freedom of choice had become the root of sin, Augustine concluded that humans are void of free will.

His position clearly contradicted earlier Christian teachings that had emphasized the importance of the freedom from bondage and the freedom of the human will, as Elaine Pagels demonstrates in *Adam, Eve, and the Serpent*. In addition, and consistent with the disapproving view of passion common among Christians at that time, Augustine defined spontaneous sexual desire as the evidence of, and the penalty for, original sin. He argued that Adam and Eve's sexual desire — and the trouble it caused — was the result of their disobedience to God, and that Adam's "sin" of copulating with Eve would itself be transmitted from generation to generation through the act of sexual intercourse. Augustine thus concluded that all descendents of Adam — basically the entire human race — was tainted and guilty of original sin from the moment of conception. Beginning life in sin and stripped of free will to do anything about it, *humans therefore couldn't do anything but sin*. This concept in turn repudiated another foundation of the early Christian message — the goodness of God's creation. Moreover, Augustine argued that human beings were not able to cure themselves of original sin. The only hope for humans to be saved from enslavement to sin and from consequent eternal damnation was God's grace. And to receive God's grace, they had to believe that *Jesus Christ had died on the cross to redeem their sins*. In support of this assertion, Augustine drew from Paul's *Letter to the Corinthians* that explained that Jesus had suffered and "died for our sins" (1 Cor. 15:3). Shocked by Jesus' untimely death, is appears likely that his early disciples, Paul included, tried to make sense of this traumatic event by attributing certain benefits to it. However, it is important to note that *no* detailed theories about the crucifixion as atonement for some "original sin" of Adam existed during Paul's time, as Karen Armstrong reminds us.

Additional Paths to Receiving God's Grace

The belief in vicarious atonement was one way of receiving God's grace, but it was not the only way. Another method was confession and the request for forgiveness. In addition, Christians had to get baptized in order to become open vessels for grace, as discussed. Infant baptism had become a widely popular practice among the Christian clergy during the time of St. Augustine. Together with the confession of sins, baptism became one of the seven official sacraments of the Church considered indispensable to wash away the stain of original sin. Any infant who died without baptism was technically destined for hell. This belief was subsequently revised. Today, the Church argues that there is hope that the souls of children who have not been baptized can be brought into eternal happiness (yet, at the same time, the Vatican paradoxically continues to stress the necessity of baptism to achieve salvation.).

Connecting the Doctrines of Original Sin and Substitutionary Atonement

While the origins of the doctrine of original sin remain controversial, since St. Augustine the hereditary transmission of original sin has become the official doctrine of the Roman Catholic Church. His teachings reinforced strict obedience to the Church and imperial authorities alike. For, if the human condition is indeed a "disease," the Church acting as the "good physician" is the indispensable vehicle for delivering the spiritual remedy and the discipline that alone can cure it.

The doctrine of original sin and its emphasis on human depravity — and indeed the corruption of *all* of nature — affected individuals by alienating them from their true Self, and thus *separating* them even further from the divine source. From a psycho-spiritual perspective, it also *disempowered* humans from playing a more proactive role as responsible co-creators in the process of evolution toward their own perfection, and toward working for a more perfected world.

St. Augustine's over-emphasis on the sinful nature of humans has left a mark on the collective psyche of Western culture. In the sixteenth century CE, the doctrine of original sin also had a considerable influence on the Protestant Reformation, most prominently on theologian John Calvin (1509-1564). Moreover, St. Augustine's interpretation of sexual desire as proof of and punishment for original sin contaminated all sexual passion with the idea of sin for centuries to come. In fact, it is probably no stretch to say that St. Augustine's interpretation led to what could be called the "unholy trinity" of guilt, shame, and fear.

St. Augustine's assumption that sexual desire naturally involves shame and guilt — because it is experienced apart from and even against our will — should be interpreted within the broader context of the Christian tradition with its predominant tendency of subordinating desire to reason, and its general emphasis on the benefits of celibacy. Already by the fourth century CE, celibates had emerged as a privileged caste within Christianity. To enter the power structure as a bishop, abbot, or theologian required a vow of celibacy. Celibate theology tends to reinforce the message that one must renounce intimate human relationships and romantic entanglements to love God utterly with an "undivided heart." However, if the path of committed relationship with a partner was chosen, sexual expression needed to be carefully managed at very least. Even some of the more liberal fathers of the Church, such as Clement of Alexandria (c. 180 CE), hence stressed that the sole legitimate purpose of marriage and sexual intercourse is to be found in procreation. At best, the Church fathers expressed deep ambivalence toward sexuality — an ambivalence that has resounded throughout Christian history for two millennia up to this day. Original sin and its unholy legacy of guilt, shame, and fear were (and still are) *not* the ideal conditions for an awakening to higher stages or structures of consciousness, nor do they encourage responsible and autonomous human participation in the workings of the sacred evolutionary impulse. Besides reinforcing the role of the Church as a mediator between God and humans, original sin served other "practical" purposes. It made the presence of evil in a world increasingly engulfed by darkness easier to understand, and answered the contentious and perennial question of why a benevolent God would allow such a gloomy state of affairs to persist. Today, Christians still widely believe that original sin explains the existence of wars, genocides, abuses, and all other atrocities in this world — a world that had originally been created in a state of perfection.

And yet, how are the doctrines of original sin and substitutionary atonement related? Even though humans could not cure themselves of original sin, St. Augustine had nevertheless offered a way out of this predicament: God's unearned grace, and a series of propositions that flow from this premise. First, the grace of God could only be received by offering the sacrifice of a *perfect human life*. Second, since the entire human race had been tainted by Adam's fall, having sinned so grievously against the will of God, no ordinary individual could possibly constitute this acceptable sacrifice. Therefore, the Son of God himself had to incarnate and offer himself as the price for Adam's sin. And, finally, only if humans believed that Jesus' death was the sacrifice for their sins, would divine forgiveness be possible.

Jesus' passion and his death were considered timeless. His sacrifice applied and continues to apply in *every generation* to his disciples, who, together with all "sinful humanity," are responsible for his death. According to the Roman catechism (published in 1566), all those must be regarded as guilty who continue to relapse into their sins. Since human transgressions made Jesus Christ suffer the torment of the cross, all those who engage in crimes crucify the Son of God anew in their hearts (for he is in them) and hold him up to contempt, according to Roman-Catholic teachings.

For God So Loved the World…

Before we examine the more problematic aspects of the doctrine of vicarious atonement, the idea of Jesus dying because of our sins can, from another point of view, be acknowledged and regarded as an expression of God's great love for humanity: "For God so loved the world that He gave his only begotten Son" (John 3:16). In other terms, our own sense of sin and guilt need not stand between us and God forever without remedy. New beginnings are possible; we need not be held in bondage by the burden of our past. Yet, when this story becomes the *predominant* or *only* story for imaging Jesus, it has serious limitations. First, this conception can lead to a *static* understanding of the Christian life, making it into a repeated cycle of sin, guilt, and forgiveness. We may be absolved each Sunday when confessing, only to sin again during the week. Progressive religious thinkers like Matthew Fox have repeatedly challenged this one-dimensional over-emphasis on sin, and the fall/redemption theology in the West, and have reminded us of how much of the person and message of Jesus Christ has, sadly, been lost as a result. Second, the doctrine of vicarious atonement encourages a *static* and *passive* understanding of the Christian life. Rather than seeing life as an evolutionary process of spiritual growth, transformation, and human participation, it focuses on the belief that God has already done what needed to be done. This conceives of God as primarily a lawgiver and judge whose strict requirements must be met. Moreover, it limits the concept of God's love by saying that God can only forgive sins if adequate recompense is made. Because we cannot meet these requirements as "fallen humans,"

God graciously provides the necessary sacrifice. Third, this doctrine leads to an understanding of Christianity as primarily a religion of *the afterlife*. The crucial issue is to believe in vicarious atonement now for the sake of salvation at a later point.

Yet, what about those who don't believe in Jesus' sacrifice for our sins? Is there any hope of salvation for them? According to official Church teachings, God will only forgive those who believe that Jesus was the sacrifice; forgiveness becomes thus conditional. Jesus Christ, however, talked about unconditional love and forgiveness that applied not just to the elected few but to *all* of humanity. And unconditional love is a mirror of God's love that is so great that "he gave his only Son." This proclamation in John doesn't have to be understood as referring to Jesus' death on the cross as substitutionary atonement for sin; it could equally be read as referring to Jesus' incarnation as *a whole*. God loves the world so much that God incarnate in Jesus became part of it, partaking of it, vulnerable to it. To love the world means to love the world as God embodied in Jesus loved it — even to the point of giving up one's life for it.

These are but a few of the more problematic aspects of the doctrine of vicarious atonement. As Richard Smoley puts it succinctly: "Did the human race so irk the Supreme Being by trespassing a minor command that it was completely alienated from him, and could God's wrath be quenched only by having a part of himself come down and offer itself as a sacrifice to another part? Put this way, the absurdity of this doctrine becomes apparent."[18]

Today, most people believe that the doctrine of vicarious

atonement is the only "official" Christian understanding of Jesus' death, and that this has been the case since the birth of Christianity. Seeing Jesus' death primarily within the framework of substitutionary atonement as an elaborate doctrine, however, goes far *beyond* what the biblical passages state. Moreover, the Gospels provide ample evidence that Jesus did not primarily die *for* the sins of the world but was rather executed *because* of the sins of the world. In other terms, because he challenged the existing domination system, he put himself in harm's way. We can thus conclude that the doctrine of vicarious atonement was largely unknown in the early centuries of Christianity. In addition, it became official Church doctrine only after the fourth century CE and gained importance only in the West.

Finally, other perceptions of Jesus' death and sacrifice exist. For example, Peter Abelard (1079-1147), the charismatic theologian and philosopher of Paris, developed a sophisticated and moving rationale for the mystery of the atonement. He argued that Christ had been crucified to awaken compassion in us for the suffering of *all* life and that by doing so he heals us. And indeed, Jesus Christ's arms stretched out along the horizontal line of the cross are an expression of that profound compassion that is also symbolized by the Bodhisattva's multiple arms reaching out to all suffering humanity in Mahayana Buddhism. It is in this compassion for the suffering of our fellow humans and all other manifestations of life that we will eventually remove our minds from blind attachment to worldly desires and turn to Christ. Viewed in this context, the suffering Christ can be a powerful catalyst for a spiritual awakening and a profound transformation.

He evokes the Christ consciousness in our hearts as the "living Christ," thus he truly becomes our savior. The path of spiritual transformation of which Jesus speaks leads to a life centered in God, as expressed in his famous proclamation "I am in the Father, and the Father (is) in me" (John 14:10-11). Father Thomas Keating speaks of Jesus on the cross, stretched out between heaven and earth, as a profound symbol of the union of matter, body, mind, soul, and spirit. Jesus is leading the way for us all to do the same. This process of divinization, as Eastern Christian traditions put it, is beautifully expressed in the liturgical prayer: "By the mystery of this water and wine, may we come to share in the divinity of Christ, who humbled himself to share in our humanity." Moreover, Huston Smith reminds us that the root meaning of the doctrine of atonement is *reconciliation*, the recovery of union and wholeness that atonement, or "at-one-ment," points toward. Early Christians were convinced that Jesus Christ's death had facilitated an unparalleled rapprochement between God and humanity to remedy the tragic estrangement that had occurred as a result of the Fall.

Another intriguing perception of Jesus' death and sacrifice comes from Jungian psychology. His crucifixion symbolizes the death of our separate self. The "sacrifice" is the arduous psycho-spiritual process we have to go through to discover who we truly are. Symbolically, the "crucifixion of the ego" involves the letting go of all illusory hopes, attachments, and distractions that offer only temporary relief from suffering. We follow the model of Jesus Christ by becoming our authentic Self.

Shut Your Mouth and Keep on Serving by George Grosz, 1927.
Art © Estate of George Grosz/Licensed by VAGA, New York, NY

Throughout time and history, the image of the suffering savior on the cross has inspired artists to create multiple variations and adaptations. One such adaptation reflecting Jesus Christ's spirit of compassion for the suffering of all life comes from the German painter George Grosz. In 1928, he depicted Christ on the cross with gas mask and soldier boots. Grosz created this image in commemoration of the millions of soldiers during World War I who were treated as cannon fodder and were sent into the trenches by the nationalistic propaganda of ruthless and irresponsible governments. An untold number of these soldiers had to endure unspeakable hardship and atrocities, with millions of them condemned to a faceless, anonymous death in the trenches.

World Tree Symbolism, Cross, and Resurrection — A Cross-Cultural View

The cross is the symbol of Christianity par excellence, to which only the symbolism of the fish or the lamb may be compared in significance. The Greek word for fish, *ichthys*, contains the initials of the Christian message "Jesus Christ, Son of God, Savior." The fish symbol served as a secret password by which Jesus' disciples could identify each other during the persecutions of the early days. And the lamb became a symbol for both the suffering (passion) and the triumphant Christ (resurrection).

The great emphasis on the cross as the primary symbol of Christianity has, however, created some controversy among scholars and religious thinkers over the last few decades. Matthew Fox has repeatedly reminded us that this emphasis is primarily a result of the fall/redemption theology commonly associated with the Christian tradition. Fox makes a strong case for a more balanced view that would equally acknowledge and honor Jesus' great *love of life in all its dimensions*. In its most basic and political meaning, the cross represents the punishment and death of a man who threatened the ruling elite by suggesting a radically new kind of society. Similarly, the expression "following the way of the cross" has frequently become synonymous with a commitment to the path of confrontation with domination systems.

Yet the cross symbolism can be seen as more multifaceted; it has its own intrinsic power that, in its origins, can be traced back to ancient times. On a mystical-esoteric level, the cross may represent the material world and the dimensions of time and space by which each one of us is held in bondage or "crucified."

It makes thus equal sense to look at the cross as an invitation to a personal path of transformation, as discussed. From a Jungian viewpoint, the cross suggests metaphorically that we die to an old way of being and that we experience a rebirth into a new way of relating to the world. In other words, the cross thus represents supreme detachment, the ultimate letting go of the fear of death. At the deepest level, it exemplifies our own spiritual journey.

The commitment to the path of personal transformation as symbolized by the cross becomes even more compelling when we consider that Jesus Christ has not always been depicted as dying on a cross in European iconography. In a Renaissance painting by an unknown Alsatian master dating back to the late 15th century, Jesus Christ is on the "Tree of Life," flanked by John the Baptist, the Apostle John, the Virgin Mary, and the Apostle Peter, among others. In this painting, it is the "living tree" that replaces the "dead wood" of the cross. The Tree of Life is a very rich and multi-layered symbol that we encounter in most of the world's cultures. The Kabbalist Tree of Life, for example, symbolizes a map of existence that reveals the structure of the universe and the evolution of human consciousness. On a personal level, the Kabbalist Tree of Life shows where we are on our journey of ascent toward the divine, and it offers us the necessary tools for overcoming obstacles and for opening us up to higher states of awareness by allowing us to reconnect with the different levels and patterns of universal energies. The *Bodhi* tree under which the Buddha attained Supreme Enlightenment is another variation of the Tree of Life. Just as Jesus Christ vanquished death, offering eternal life to all those who would follow the "way

Christ on the Tree of Life, painting by Alsatian Master, 3rd quarter 15th Century. Photo, museums of Strasbourg, France

of the cross," so too did the Buddha transcend the endless cycle of life, death, and rebirth, or *samsara*, after attaining liberation from all suffering. In another example from Nordic mythology, we are told that the god Odin voluntarily hung himself for nine days on the World Tree, *Yggdrasil*, to acquire the wisdom of the runes, the magic letters of the Nordic alphabet.

    The Tree of Life is the pivotal Tree of the Universe, the World Axis, from which the four directions radiate. This understanding is also consistent with Mesoamerican cosmology that synthesized the World Tree symbolism with the Christian cross after the Spanish conquest. This fusion suggests that in Mesoamerican understanding the new Christian cross still retained much of its ancient significance as the center of the cosmos. The cross has also been symbolically represented at the center of Tibetan mandalas and Native American medicine wheels. Moreover, in *The Mayan Calendar and the Transformation of Consciousness,* Carl Johan Calleman argues that the World Tree has a number of holographic micro-projections on the human body where it forms the basis of the chakra system and the various meridians of Eastern medicine. Through the World Tree, this energy of life, called *qi* or *prana* depending on the tradition, is related to the creative fields of the entire universe.

    In addition, the image of Jesus Christ hanging on the Tree of Life conveys a message that reveals archetypal similarity with pagan vegetation deities. In fact, even within the Christian tradition some allusions to the "green nature" of Christ can be found. This imagery is strongly evoked in the Gospel of John when Mary Magdalene mistakes the newly risen Christ for the "gardener" (20:15). The work of the gardener is to nurture vegetation — a primary role of what is known in the pagan tradition as the "Green Man." Jesus Christ's own association with *some* aspects of this symbolism is expressed in statements such as "I am the true vine" (John 15:1), "I am the bread of life" (John 6:35), and "I am the good shepherd" (John 10:11). These statements are reminiscent of the pre-Christian gods Dionysus (Greek god of the grape known in Rome as Bacchus), Dumuzi/Tammuz (Mesopotamian vegetation god, also referred to as "Divine Shepherd"), and Attis (vegetation god of Asia minor, or modern-day Turkey). Dumuzi and Attis were both the son and lover of the Goddess in her forms as Inanna/Ishtar and Kybele. The central theme of Christianity, the crucifixion and resurrection, corresponds to these ancient Mediterranean and Near Eastern vegetation narratives that celebrated the death and rebirth of the "Green Man," the dying and resurrected vegetation god, of whom many versions were known.

The major event of the Christian liturgy — the transubstantiation of the bread and wine into the body and blood of Christ — is reminiscent of the sacrificial act of Dumuzi, the god of the grain (body), and Dionysus, the god of wine (blood). Pre-Christian cultures commonly viewed the sacrifice as a gift to the mysterious source of life that would cause a seed to germinate. The same sacrificial theme can be found in the narrative of the death and resurrection of Osiris in ancient Egypt. Osiris had originally been a deity of vegetation and agriculture, hence ensuring abundant harvests. Osiris also became king of Egypt. He introduced humankind to the arts of civilization and taught people how to make bread and wine. Many festivals were held in Osiris' honor. However, his younger brother Seth grew jealous of his popularity and plotted his death. He killed Osiris and scattered his body parts over Egypt. Yet Osiris' loving consort, the goddess Isis, found the parts and restored Osiris to life. Eventually, the resurrected god became the ruler of the dead and a powerful symbol of immortality. The dead Osiris representing the regenerative powers of the natural world was sometimes depicted with corn growing from his body, flanked by inscriptions of the *ankh* cross, the symbol of eternal life. In a ritual aimed at obtaining immortality, Egyptians would consume his "flesh" in the form of "communion cakes" made of wheat — a striking resemblance to the Eucharist. Similarly, the "flesh" and "blood" of the Greek "god man" Dionysus — who died with the coming of winter and was always brought back to life in spring — were ritually consumed in the form of bread and wine. In pre-Christian cultures, life and death were perceived as being intertwined. Life would arise from death, as it manifests itself most profoundly in the vegetative cycle of the seasons.

In addition to the omnipresent image of Christ suffering and dying on the cross, the symbolic representation of Christ on the Tree of Life is of great value because it offers a more balanced and life-affirming perspective that is consistent with the serious ecological challenges of our time. In an age in which the ecological devastation of Gaia, the earth, is forcing humanity to reevaluate its relationship to the natural world, this image holds the potential that may overcome the traditional dualistic view of mainstream Christian theology. For many centuries, the image of a transcendent God *separate* from the "fallen" world of humankind and "corrupted" nature has reinforced the notion of humankind's dominion over nature, opening the door to excessive exploitation of natural resources and all other life forms. At this critical juncture in time and history, the archetypal image of a greener and more life-affirming Christ can serve as a source of inspiration for an ecological Christian spirituality that honors nature as an equally beautiful manifestation of the divine. Christ on the Tree of Life is an embodiment of the creative life force that causes trees to leaf, flowers to blossom, and plants to bear fruit. Viewed in this context, Jesus Christ truly becomes the "resurrection and the life" (John 11:25), the way from death to immortality. He embodies the essence of life and growth that has always been associated with Mother Nature. Matthew Fox talks about the "cosmic Christ" who is fully present to all of creation. This is a Christ who *celebrates and proclaims life rather than death.* Moreover, it is a Christ who embodies a new creation, a glorious new birth: "I have come that they may have life, and may have it in all its fullness" (John 10:10).

The theme of death and rebirth — the central drama in Christianity — is a common motif in all of the world's cultures. Another striking parallel to the Christian passion and resurrection story can be found in the legend of the most prominent savior figure of Mesoamerican eschatological mythology: Quetzalcoatl, which translates to "plumed serpent." Quetzalcoatl was the name given to him by the Aztecs. To the Mayas of Yucatan he was known as Kukulcan. In the jungles of Guatemala at Palenque, a Mayan temple known as the "Temple of the Cross" exhibits a cross that is symbolically affiliated with the archetypal savior Kukulcan/Quetzalcoatl. As a savior-hero with white skin complexion and a beard — a fatal physical resemblance with the Spanish conquerors — Quetzalcoatl was believed to have played an important part in creation, and to have introduced his people to the arts of civilization. However, in its deeper esoteric meaning, the narrative of Quetzalcoatl bears a certain resemblance to some of the fundamental aspects of the Christian passion and resurrection drama. Born of a virgin, Quetzalcoatl eventually renounced the material riches he had enjoyed as a ruler and offered himself as a sacrifice by throwing himself into a funeral pyre. After having been consumed by the fire, he underwent an archetypal journey of transformation by venturing into the Land of the Dead. There he obtained the bones of a man and a woman whom he redeemed with his own blood. We are told that Quetzalcoatl then ascended to the heavens where he merged with Venus, the morning and evening star. Quetzalcoatl's story became an archetypal expression of the universal theme of death and resurrection, sin and redemption, and of the transfiguration of a human into a god. His death, his journey through the underworld, and his rebirth all display the essential motif found in all of the great wisdom traditions: the incarnation of the infinite un-manifest Spirit into the manifest world of form and the agonizing redemption of matter by Spirit. Spirit is subject to the laws of the physical realm that it consciously enters. The ensuing paradox, the infinite bound in the finite, engenders a fundamental tension that can never be fully resolved. Once this tension reaches a breaking point — exemplified by the agony of Jesus' crucifixion and Quetzalcoatl's self-immolation on the funeral pyre — the embodied manifestation is shattered in death only to rise again in a transfigured state. This is a process that unfolds, again and again, in all dimensions — from the life cycle of a tiny insect to the birth and death of an entire galaxy. The union of opposite principles is also represented in Quetzalcoatl's name (i.e., "Feathered Serpent") that fuses the images of the earthbound serpent and a bird's flight.

The figure of Quetzalcoatl is affiliated with the Mayan "Temple of the Cross." A bird is exhibited at the top of the Mayan cross, similar to the dove symbolizing the Holy Spirit, and at the base of the cross we find a death mask that bears some resemblance to the skull of Adam in Christian iconography. In many paintings of the crucifixion, Jesus' blood falls on the skull of Adam. According to Christian belief, his blood retroactively baptizes the first man and with him the entire human race.

The agony of Jesus' crucifixion and the apotheosis of his resurrection are reminiscent of the classical mythological pattern of the archetypal journey of the savior-hero who descends to the underworld, redeems fallen humanity, and transcends death and mortality through his sacrificial act. After his death, according to Christian tradition, Jesus descended to the underworld. There he harrowed hell and symbolically redeemed Adam, Eve, and all the doomed souls, indicating that through him the ancient "original sin" and the ensuing death could be overcome. On a deeper esoteric level, the Harrowing of Hell is an interesting interlude in the passion drama as it shows Jesus shining the non-judgmental and harmonizing light of consciousness even into the deepest places of darkness and suffering. The meaning of his passage through these realms is to release hell from the agonizing grip of duality and to hold *all* of its boundary conditions in love's infinite embrace. On the third day after his death Jesus rose from the grave and conversed with his followers. Forty days later he ascended to heaven, thereby completing the cycle of return from the Land of the Dead that culminated in his final apotheosis, thus marking the climax of the archetypal journey of the savior-hero in much the same fashion as we can observe in the savior-hero narrative as it appears across the world's cultures.

Conclusion

To take Jesus Christ seriously is to follow him. To follow him is to participate in his passion. And his passion is a life centered in God and his teachings of the Kingdom of God — an alternative social vision of a transformed world without violence, war, discrimination, and injustice. Jesus' vision also implies a world of abundance, of "milk and honey," without lack and scarcity. Moreover, it is a society of fully awakened and compassionate humans who follow the "way of the cross" by putting love into action and engaging in selfless service. And it is a world in which human consciousness has internalized the profound meaning of interrelatedness on a collective scale by transcending separation and all dualist notions. Finally, it is a world in which humans are spiritually empowered and fully conscious of their inherent potential to actively and creatively shape the divine evolutionary impulse as responsible and engaged co-creators.

Jesus' subversion of all forms of authority and worldly power harbors a vast potential for fundamental change on every level. He is a boundary-smasher who calls people to step outside their comfort zones for the sake of love and justice. To walk the path of Christ means to seek divinity not externally but at the deepest core of our being. The radical intensity of the "way of the cross" has the power to transform people at the heart level. It leads to a life in God and participation in the passion of God as known and revealed in Jesus of Nazareth. Jesus' transfiguration and his realization of fundamental unity with God has a unique and poignant urgency for our time. As a teacher of non-dual wisdom Jesus models for us what it means "to make the two become one." By being both fully human and fully divine, Jesus Christ unites our two natures. Ultimately, his existence tells the story of the divine manifesting in a human body, so that humans may fully awaken to their own divine potential by following his inspirational example. The agony of his crucifixion and the mystery of his glorious resurrection help us to recognize that there is no Easter without Good Friday. By being pierced willingly, Jesus gave birth, literally and metaphysically, to a sacred new creation. He came not to found a new religion or to inaugurate a new set of dogmas but to introduce a revolutionary new path of love in action. And this path still harbors the potential to save humanity from its current course of self-destruction.

In the centuries after Jesus' death, the Christian cross became a symbol for the static masculine archetype as represented by the tradition of the imperial Church. Though Jesus had been a "prophet of the heart," the cross upon which he was crucified was firmly planted in the soil of the Roman Empire that, in its values, was anything but loving. Jesus' message of love and his promise of redemption in a world of paradoxes was adjusted and partly changed to serve the power needs of an institution that was authoritarian, patriarchal, and hierarchical in its structures. As Christianity spread through the Roman Empire and became the official state religion at the end of the fourth century CE, it adopted the imperial values of control and domination. The lines of the cross were now becoming transformed into a symbol of rigid boundaries and sharp distinctions, separating male from female, good from evil, rationality from intuition, logos from eros, and spirit from body. In the late eleventh century CE and throughout the Middle Ages and beyond, the cross was even co-opted as a rallying sign by crusaders who waged "holy wars" of extermination against Muslims, Jews, and all those who were regarded as heretics because they challenged the official doctrine of the Roman-Catholic Church. Jesus was now given the role of the "warrior Christ" who waged just wars for the sake of his people against all "unbelievers." This perception of Jesus reflected a narrow ethnocentric consciousness of exclusivity that clearly repudiated the compassionate, inclusive, and universal message of a more world-centric Christ. Yet, despite such abuses down through the centuries, what Jesus modeled for humanity has stood the test of time. Jesus' message of unconditional love, forgiveness, and unity among *all* people has lived on in great mystics and saints such as St. Francis, Meister Eckhart, St. Teresa of Avila, Mother Theresa, Martin Luther King, Father Thomas Keating and Brother David Steindl-Rast. Jesus continues to inspire the lives of everyday people who are living embodiments of his timeless message by their inspired efforts to make this world a better place.

Bibliography

Quotations from the Christian canonical and non-canonical scriptures are taken from the *Revised English Bible* (Oxford/Cambridge University Press, 1989), from the *Restored New Testament* (New York & London: Norton & Co., 2009), translated by Willis Barnstone, and from the *International Edition of the Nag Hammadi Scriptures* (New York: HarperOne, 2007), edited by Marvin Meyer, which is the revised and updated translation of Gnostic texts.

Adams, James Rowe. *From Literal to Literary. The Essential Reference Book for Biblical Metaphor.* Bend OR: Rising Star Press, 2005.

Amis, Robin. *A Different Christianity.* Albany, NY: SUNY Press, 1995.

Anderson, William. *Green Man: The Archetype of our Oneness with the Earth.* San Francisco: HarperCollins, 1990.

Armstrong, Karen. *A History of God: The 4,000-Year Quest of Judaism, Christianity, and Islam.* New York: Ballantine Books, 1993.

Aslan, Reza. *Zealot: The Life and Times of Jesus of Nazareth.* New York: Random House, 2013.

Baring, Anne, and Jules Cashford. *The Myth of the Goddess: Evolution of an Image.* London: Arkana (Penguin Books), 1991.

Borg, Marcus. *Jesus: Uncovering the Life, Teachings, and Relevance of a Religious Revolutionary.* New York: HarperOne, 2006.

___. *The Heart of Christianity.* New York: HarperCollins, 2004.

___. *Meeting Jesus Again for the First Time.* New York: HarperOne, 1994.

Bourgeault, Cynthia. *The Wisdom Jesus: Transforming Heart and Mind — A New Perspective on Christ and His Message.* Boston&London: Shambhala, 2008.

Buehrens, John. *Understanding the Bible: An Introduction for Skeptics, Seekers, and Religious Liberals.* Boston: Beacon Press, 2003.

Bynum, Caroline Walker. *The Resurrection of the Body in Western Christianity.* New York: Columbia University Press, 1995.

Calleman, Carl Johan. *The Mayan Calendar and the Transformation of Consciousness.* Rochester, Vermont: Bear & Co, 2004.

Campbell, Joseph. *Thou Art That: Transforming Religious Metaphor.* Novato, CA: New World Library, 2001.

Eliade, Mircea, and Couliano, Ioan. *Concise Guide to World Religions* (Christian Religion, p.58-89). HarperSanFrancisco, 1991.

Ehrman, Bart. *Jesus, Interrupted: Revealing the Hidden Contradictions in the Bible (and Why We Don't Know About Them).* New York: HarperOne, 2009.

___. *Lost Christianities: The Battle for Scripture and the Faiths We Never Knew.* New York: Oxford University Press, 2003.

Fox, Matthew. *The Coming of the Cosmic Christ.* San Francisco: HarperCollins, 1980.

___. *Creation Spirituality: Liberating Gifts for the Peoples of the Earth.* HarperSanFrancisco, 1991.

___. *Original Blessing.* New York: Tarcher/Putnam, edition 2000.

Frazer, James. *The Golden Bough.* New York: Macmillan Publishing Co.,1963.

Freyne, Sean. "The Geography, Politics and Economics of Galilee." In *Studying the Historical Jesus: Evaluations of the State of Current Research.* Leiden: Brill, 1994.

Harvey, Andrew. *The Essential Mystics,* New Jersey: Castle Books, 1998.

Johnson, Luke Timothy. *The Writings of the New Testament: An Interpretation,* revised edition with the assistance of Todd Penner, Minneapolis: Fortress Press, 1999.

Keating, Thomas, *Intimacy with God*, New York: Crossroad, 1994.
___. *The Mystery of Christ*. Rockport, MA: Element Books, 1987.
King, Karen L. *The Gospel of Mary of Magdala: Jesus and the First Woman Apostle*. Santa Rosa, CA: Polebridge, 2003.
Leeming, David. *Jealous Gods and Chosen People: The Mythology of the Middle East*. New York: Oxford University Press, 2004.
Levenson, Jon D. *Death and Resurrection of the Beloved Son: The Transformation of Child Sacrifice in Judaism and Christianity*. New Haven: Yale University Press, 1993.
Marion, Jim. *Putting on the Mind of Christ: The Inner Work of Christian Spirituality*. Charlottesville, VA: Hampton Roads Publishing, 2000.
McGehee, Pittman J., and Thomas, Damon J. *The Invisible Church: Finding Spirituality Where You Are*. Westport, CT: Praeger Publishers, 2009.
Meyer, Marvin. *The Gnostic Discoveries*. HarperSanFrancisco, 2005.
Meyers, Robin. *The Underground Church: Reclaiming the Subversive Way of Jesus*. San Francisco, CA: Jossey-Bass Books (Wiley), 2012.
Needleman, Jacob. *Lost Christianity*. Garden City, NY: Doubleday, 1980.
Pagels, Elaine. *The Gnostic Gospels*. New York: Vintage Books Edition, 1989.
___. Adam, Eve, and the Serpent. New York: Vintage Books Edition, 1989.
Panikkar, Raimon. *Christophany: The Fullness of Man*. Maryknoll, NY: Orbis Books, 2004.
Radford Ruether, Rosemary. *Goddesses and the Divine Feminine*, University of California Press, 2005.
___. Christianity. In *Women in World Religions*, edited by Arvind Sharma p. 207-233. Albany: State University of New York Press, 1987.
Reynolds, Stephen. *The Christian Religious Tradition*, Encino, CA: Dickenson 1977.

Rohr, Richard. *Things Hidden: Scripture as Spirituality.* Cincinnati, OH: St. Anthony Messenger Press, 2008.

____. *The Search for our True Self.* San Francisco, CA: Jossey-Bass Books (Wiley), 2013.

Sanford, John A. *The Kingdom Within: The Inner Meaning of Jesus' Sayings.* New York: HarperCollins, 1987.

Sanguin, Bruce. *The Emerging Church: A Model for Change and a Map for Renewal,* Woodlake Publishing Inc., 2008.

Shapiro, Rami. *The Divine Feminine in Biblical Wisdom Literature.* Woodstock, VT: SkyLight Paths, 2005.

Smith, Huston. *The World's Religions,* HarperSanFrancisco, 1991.

____. *The Soul of Christianity.* HarperSanFrancisco, 2005.

Smoley, Richard. *Inner Christianity,* Boston & London: Shambhala, 2002.

Stark, Rodney. *Discovering God.* New York: HarperOne, 2007.

Steindl-Rast, David. *Essential Writings* (Modern Spiritual Masters Series), edited by Clare Hallward. Maryknoll, NY: Orbis Books, 2010.

Vermes, Geza. *Jesus the Jew.* London: Fontana 1976.

Walker, Ethan. *The Mystic Christ.* Norman, OK: Devi Press, 2003.

Wilber, Ken. *Integral Spirituality.* Boston, MA: Shambhala, 2006.

Yogananda, Paramhansa. *Autobiography of a Yogi.* New York, 1946.

Glossary

Archetypes: Original patterns, forms, and shared memories in the collective unconscious of humankind that are often related to deities, according to the Jungian school of psychology

Bible: The Hebrew Bible is known in the Christian tradition as the "Old Testament." The "New Testament," or Christian Bible, includes the four canonical Gospels; the Acts of the Apostles; the letters of Paul and other authors; and the Book of Revelation

Catholic: Universal

Canonical: Official biblical texts of Christianity ("canonical books") that comprise the New Testament and were approved by the Church (as opposed to the non-canonical books that were left out such as the Gospel of Thomas)

Communion: The part of the Eucharist where bread and wine are consecrated and shared (Holy Communion)

Creed: A statement of faith or belief

Dogma: A principle or set of principles laid down by an authority as the indisputable truth. In Christianity, these principles are defined by the Church and viewed as the "paths leading to God"

Esoteric: Hidden or internal dimension of religion. Knowledge that allows for *inner* transformation and the exploration of different levels of consciousness (i.e., *Esoteric* Christianity)

Eucharist: Related to the Greek word for "thanksgiving." A common name for Holy Communion or the Lord's Supper

Exoteric: External dimension of religion concerned primarily with the preservation of institutions, canonical laws, ritual and liturgy (i.e., *Exoteric* Christianity)

Gnosticism: The word is derived from the Greek *gnosis*, or "knowledge." Gnosticism is based on the belief that salvation is attainable through a secret mystical knowledge

Gospel: Greek for "good news." The term commonly refers to the four canonical Gospels (Matthew, Mark, Luke, and John) that are part of the New Testament

Holy Spirit: The New Testament speaks of God as the Holy Spirit. Most Christians view the Holy Spirit (symbolized by a dove) as the third "person" of the Holy Trinity

Holy Week: Palm Sunday marks the beginning. On Thursday, Jesus institutes the Last Supper, after which he is arrested. On Good Friday he is crucified, and on Easter Sunday he is said to have risen from the dead

Incarnation: The divine embodied in human form. In traditional Christian understanding, Jesus Christ is viewed as the one and only incarnation of God. As the "Son of the Father," he is seen as the second "person" of the Holy Trinity

Integral Theory: Based on the pioneering work of philosopher Ken Wilber who synthesized the findings of modern scientific research and developmental psychology with the world's wisdom traditions

Liturgy: The act of public worship as characteristic of Christian church services

Messiah: The term is derived from the Hebrew *moshiach*, which means the "anointed one" (translated into Greek as *khristos* and anglicized as Christ). Christianity claims that Jesus is the prophesied Messiah and redeemer of humankind

Mysticism: Focus is on accessing the Absolute in the most direct and immediate way without mediation by religious institutions. A mystic is a person who has attained union with the Divine

Myth: An ancient tale based on oral tradition. The term derives from

Greek *musteion* (i.e., to "close one's eyes and mouth"), and is etymologically related to the words mystery and mysticism

Nicene Creed: The Church Council at Nicaea (325CE) – together with the Church Council of Chalcedon (451CE) – introduced the threefold theology about Father, Son, and Holy Spirit ("three-in-one, yet undivided"), which is reflected in the Trinitarian dogma

Orthodoxy: Term refers literally to the "correct" or "right teaching." In the Christian tradition, this word was commonly used to distinguish between those who adhered to the officially approved theological teachings of the Church versus those who did not

Pentecost: This celebration commemorates the day when Jesus' disciples received inspiration by the Holy Spirit (symbolized by tongues of fire representing different languages). Christianity claims that they were given the authority to proclaim the "good news" to all the people and nations

Sacrament: An "external" and visible sign of an "internal" and spiritual grace. The two primary sacraments are baptism and Holy Communion

Spiral Dynamics: A spiral-shaped model of psychosocial development that is mostly based on the pioneering work of psychologist Clare Graves

Torah: Hebrew term that means both "law" and "teaching." Traditionally known as the "Five Books of Moses" or the Pentateuch in Greek. The Torah contains both ethical-moral injunctions and the foundational stories of Judaism

Transubstantiation: In Roman Catholic teachings the mystical process by which the consecrated host and wine are transformed into the very body and blood of the Christ

Footnotes

1. Today's movement for Integral Christianity unites the profound wisdom of the Christian esoteric tradition with the leading-edge integral map of human consciousness and development through stages and states, and in so doing offers a progressive vision of hope for the twenty-first century. This vision has, most prominently, been explored and expounded by renowned Christian contemplatives Father Thomas Keating and Brother David Steindl-Rast, and by integral philosopher Ken Wilber.
2. Smith, *The World's Religions*, p. 318.
3. Borg, *Meeting Jesus Again for the First Time*, p. 25.
4. Freyne, *The Geography, Politics and Economics of Galilee*, p. 76.
5. Smoley, *Inner Christianity*, p. 213.
6. Smith, *The World's Religions*, p. 320.
7. Ehrman, *Jesus, Interrupted*, p. 164.
8. Smith, *The World's Religions*, p. 321.
9. Smoley, *Inner Christianity*, p. 155.
10. Ruether, *Women in World Religions*, p. 218.
11. Harvey, *The Essential Mystics*, p. 170.
12. Smith, *The Soul of Christianity*, p. 59.
13. Keating, *Intimacy with God*, p. 163.
14. Borg, *Meeting Jesus Again for the First Time*, p. 56.
15. Armstrong, *A History of God*, p. 83.
16. Borg, Jesus: *Uncovering the Life, Teachings, and Relevance of a Religious Revolutionary*, p. 276.
17. Smith, *The Soul of Christianity*, p. 74.
18. Smoley, *Inner Christianity*, p. 132.

www.ingramcontent.com/pod-product-compliance
Lightning Source LLC
Chambersburg PA
CBHW071923290426
44110CB00013B/1459